Nineteenth annual report on monitoring the application of Community law

2001

European Commission

Each year the European Commission draws up a report on the monitoring of the application of Community law, in response to requests made by the European Parliament (resolution of 9 February 1983) and the Member States (point 2 of Declaration No 19 annexed to the Treaty signed at Maastricht on 7 February 1992). The report also responds to the requests expressed by the European Council or the Council in relation to specific sectors.

Per
ZZ
EM112
A60

A great deal of additional information on the European Union is available on the Internet.
It can be accessed through the Europa server (http://europa.eu.int).

Cataloguing data can be found at the end of this publication.

Luxembourg: Office for Official Publications of the European Communities, 2002

ISBN 92-894-4114-3

Printed in Italy

Contents

Contents

1. INTRODUCTION

Whereas, as the White Paper published by the Commission in 2001 also emphasises, prime responsibility for applying Community law lies with national administrations and courts, it falls to the Commission to monitor the transposal of Community law where necessary, the compatibility with Community law of the national provisions transposing that law and the proper application of Community law by various bodies in the Member States.

The White Paper on European Governance points out that the impact of Community law 'depends on the willingness and capacity of Member State authorities to ensure that they are transposed and enforced effectively, fully and on time'.

The Commission's activity in monitoring the application of Community law covers Community law in its entirety. As such, it is not unusual for the Commission to take action against a Member State for adopting or maintaining legislation or rules which are contrary to the fundamental principles of Community law as enshrined in the Treaties.

Within this framework, cooperation between administrative bodies in the Member States and the Commission forms a vital component of the Commission's remit, as vested in it by the Treaties, to act as the guardian of Community law.

In this spirit the Commission seeks to promote, at all stages of infringement proceedings, contacts between its departments and the national administrations. The primary objective of infringement proceedings (Article 226 EC and Article 141 Euratom), particularly in the pre-litigation stage, is to encourage the Member State involved to comply voluntarily with Community law as quickly as possible. Optimal exploitation of the pre-litigation stage is thus the best way of achieving the objectives vested in the Commission by the Treaties.

This duty of cooperation is formally enshrined in Article 10 of the EC Treaty.

The Commission was obliged to activate these provisions on 20 occasions in 2001 when Member States had failed to cooperate on infringement proceedings. Eight of these sets of proceedings were still ongoing at 31 December 2001. This represents an increase in relation to 2000, when only seven sets of proceedings were started under Article 10; four of them were still ongoing at 31 December 2001.

However, the Commission starts Article 10 proceedings only where the Member State in question has repeatedly failed to cooperate; as such, these figures do not include delays in processing files which result from national administrations taking excessive time to reply within the framework of infringement proceedings. The Article 10 procedure is not necessary – and therefore is not used – where the Commission has the information needed to proceed to the next stage of proceedings.

This is why it is vital for the Commission to have the information it needs to carry out its duties, including outside the framework of direct contact with the authorities of the Member States.

The numerous complaints received from European citizens constitute essential information which enables the Commission to carry out its duties properly. In the interest of ensuring the greatest possible transparency in the management of complaints submitted by citizens, the Commission is to publish in 2002 a consolidated version of the administrative measures it takes in its relations with complainants in respect of alleged infringements of Community law.

The nineteenth annual report on monitoring the application of Community law reports on the Commission's activities in connection with monitoring the application of Community law in 2001.

With a view to addressing Parliament's call in its resolution on the eighteenth annual report for a more analytical, less descriptive approach to the Commission's work in this field, this report places the Commission's monitoring of the application of Community law, where possible, in the context of the Community's political and legislative programme.

A general description of the use made by the Commission of the infringement procedure as a prelude to formal proceedings takes the following form:

– a statistical overview showing the various stages involved in monitoring the application of Community law and statistical trends in relation to the previous year (point 1.1);
– improvements in the pre-litigation procedure (point 1.2);

- transposal by the Member States of Community directives (point 1.3);
- applications for derogations from harmonisation measures – Article 95 of the EC Treaty; this section is in response to Parliament's requests (point 1.4);
- application of the international agreements adopted by the Community and the law derived from those agreements; this section is in response to Parliament's request (point 1.5);
- a graphical overview, by Member State, of all the infringement proceedings commenced or handled by the Commission during 2001 (point 1.6);
- an overview of the use made by the Commission, since entry into force of the Maastricht Treaty, of the penalty mechanism provided for in Article 228 of the EC Treaty (point 1.7).

1.1. Statistics for 2001

The statistics for 2001 reflect, once again, a degree of stability in the number of complaints registered by the Commission: up slightly on 2000 but still below the number recorded in 1999. Complaints still form the bulk of infringement proceedings initiated by the Commission against the Member States, and a corresponding decline is observed in the number of cases opened by the Commission on the basis of its own investigations.

The statistics for 2001 can be summed up as follows.

- The total number of infringement cases initiated by the Commission is down 11.65 %, the lowest figure since 1999.
- The number of complaints registered by the Commission increased in 2001 (6.12 % up on 2000) but remains slightly below the 1999 record. In 2001 complaints accounted for six infringement cases out of 10 initiated by the Commission in that year.

  Inversely, the Commission opened a smaller number of cases based on its own investigations than in previous years. In 2001 there were 273 such cases, excluding infringement proceedings for failure to communicate national transposal measures.

  The number of proceedings for failure to notify is down to the lowest level since 1996.
- 1 050 letters of formal notice were issued in 2001, 25.43 % down on 2000, when 1 317 notifications were registered. However, it should be emphasised that because the backlog in operations for the issue of formal notice had been cleared by the beginning of 2000, the particularly high number of letters of formal notice

based on failure to communicate national transposal measures had inflated the year's figures. The 2001 figure should therefore be compared with the 1999 figure (1075), suggesting a degree of stability.

It should be noted that the time necessary for operations for the issue of formal notice based on failure to notify had been considerably reduced in 2000 and that this trend continued in 2001 thanks to the continued development of the Asmodée II 'directives' database.

- The number of reasoned opinions rose in 2001 from 460 to 569, an increase of 23.7 %. However, reasoned opinions as a proportion of outstanding files remains stable (27.80 % in 2001 against 23.76 % in 2000). The sudden upturn in 2001 therefore seems to be largely due to the considerable increase in the speed of notification to Member States (reduced from 29 calendar days to approximately 24 hours on average): thus, for the first time, the reasoned opinions issued in December 2001 were notified during that same year. Accordingly, the figures for 2001 represent the total number of reasoned opinions issued in December 2000 and those issued in December 2001. Only by examining the 2002 figures can the trend be determined.
- The number of cases referred to the Court of Justice fell by 5.82 %, from 172 in 2000 to 162 in 2001. But this slight decrease must be seen against the higher number of reasoned opinions in 2001 and the reduction in processing times for reasoned opinion decisions and referral decisions. The rate of referrals is fairly stable (up from 9.77 to 10.33 %).
- Processing times have increased slightly for letters of notice, 73 % of them relating to infringement proceedings commenced in 2001. But they are down for reasoned opinions, with only 23 % of reasoned opinions served concerning proceedings commenced in that year, against 14 % in 2000. However, the slight increase in processing times for letters of notice must be relativised in view of the significant number of letters of formal notice based on failure to notify issued in 2000; the opening of those files is linked to notification of the letter of formal notice; the only element of complaint, i.e. failure to notify, is established purely on the basis that the deadline for transposal has passed. But overall, processing times have not increased. Whereas 49 % of cases opened in 2000 were still pending at 31 December 2000, as at 31 December 2001 the corresponding figure for files opened in 2001 was 45.77 %.
- At the same time, the efficiency of the pre-litigation procedure was confirmed by the number of termination decisions, which stabilised at 1 915 in 2001 (1 899 in 2000);

• Lastly, the Commission's policy of transparency intensified in 2000, chiefly through greater use of the Internet as a means of disseminating information (see below). Since 17 January 2001, the Commission has announced all recent decisions to issue letters of formal notice and reasoned opinions, to refer cases to the Court of Justice and to terminate cases on the Secretariat-General's Europa web site at:
http://europa.eu.int/comm/secretariat_general/sgb/droit_com/index_en.htm#infractions
All this information is now freely accessible, whereas it used to be available only to the Member State concerned. The Commission also issued 93 press releases in 2001.

1.2. Improvements in the pre-litigation procedure

The two main improvements to infringement proceedings in 2001 concern compliance with decisions and arrangements for notifying them.

• As stated in the eighteenth annual report, the Commission has sought to reduce the time elapsing between the adoption of its infringement decisions and their notification to the Member States. Thus the streamlining work carried out reduced the time taken to issue letters of formal notice and reasoned opinions to the Member States concerned via their Permanent Representation from 29 days to 24 hours.

This was made possible by creating standard models for letters of formal notice and reasoned opinions and streamlining administrative procedures between the decision and its notification.
The time taken to comply with referral decisions has also been reduced, but this is less significant. In most cases this serves for the last contacts with the Member State concerned in a bid to encourage voluntary alignment rather than refer the matter to the Court of Justice.

• Improvements to infringement proceedings were also designed to increase the *transparency of decisions* adopted by the Commission in the field. As stated in the previous report, all recent decisions to issue letters of formal notice and reasoned opinions, to refer cases to the Court of Justice and to terminate cases are now available on the Secretariat-General's Europa server at:
http://europa.eu.int/comm/secretariat_general/sgb/droit_com/index_en.htm #infractions.
Making this information available on the Internet makes it more accessible to the general public and encourages a 'peer pressure' effect between Member States.

The frequency of Internet updates was also increased; as of July 2001 they take place every six months.

1.3. Transposal of directives

The table below gives an overall picture of the rate of notification of national measures implementing all the directives applicable on 31 December 2001.

Ranking 2001	Ranking 2000	Member State	Directives applicable on reference date	Directives for which implementing measure have been notified	Percentage notification rate on 31.12.2001	Percentage notification rate on 31.12.2000
1	1	Denmark	1 479	1 468	99.26	98.46
2	2	Spain	1 479	1 457	98.51	97.99
3	5	Sweden	1 482	1 459	98.45	97.45
4	4	Finland	1 488	1 462	98.25	97.66
5	13	Italy	1 484	1 449	97.64	95.65
6	8	Netherlands	1 486	1 448	97.44	96.66
7	10	Luxembourg	1 480	1 441	97.36	96.18
8	11	Ireland	1 477	1 437	97.29	95.90
9	3	Belgium	1 485	1 444	97.24	97.86
10	12	Portugal	1 486	1 444	97.17	95.72
11	6	Germany	1 487	1 440	96.84	96.86
12	14	France	1 485	1 437	96.77	95.05
13	15	Greece	1 478	1 428	96.62	93.95
14	7	United Kingdom	1 482	1 428	96.36	96.85
15	9	Austria	1 480	1 420	95.95	96.58
		EU-15	1 483	1 444	97.41	96.59

As at 31 December 2001 the Member States had on average notified 97.41 % of the national measures needed to implement the directives. This figure represents a clear improvement in the transposal situation in 2000 (96.59 %) and is the highest rate achieved since 1992.

However, this average rate is below the target of 98.5 % set by the Stockholm European Council for the transposal of internal market legislation. In terms of all Community legislation for transposal, only Denmark and Spain have reached that target.

The following table provides an overview of the situation for each Member State.

The summary table at the end of Part 2 of Annex IV to this report (Volume V) shows the detailed transposal rate for each Member State and each sector in 2001.

1.4. Applications for derogations from harmonisation measures – Article 95 of the EC Treaty

Article 95(a) to (b) gives Member States the possibility to maintain or introduce national provisions derogating from harmonisation measures adopted at Community level where this is justified by fundamental requirements, in particular the protection of health or the environment. The Treaty requires the Commission to approve or reject notifications submitted to it within a six-month period. When justified by the complexity of the matter and in the absence of danger for human health, the Commission may extend this period by a further six months.

In 2001, a total of seven notifications under Article 95(a) and (b) were submitted by the Member States. They concerned a German notification under Article 95(5) with regard to new national provisions going beyond the measures of Directive 1999/51/EC (prohibiting the marketing and use of organo-stannic compounds when acting as biocides in free association antifouling paint), a German notification under Article 95(4) with regard to maintaining national provisions derogating from Directive 2000/38/EC (remodelling the pharmaco-vigilance systems), a Netherlands notification under Article 95(5) with regard to new national provisions going beyond the measures of Directive 94/60/EC (harmonising amongst other things the use and marketing of creosote and similar tar distillates, as well as preparations containing them, by limiting the content of B(a)P), a UK notification under Article 95(4) with regard to maintaining national provisions going beyond the measures of Directive 98/79/EC (harmonising the rules for placing on the market and putting into service *in vitro* diagnostic medical devices), and Austrian, Finnish and Swedish notifications under Article 95(4) with regard to maintaining national provisions derogating from Directive 76/116/EEC as last amended by Directive 98/97/EC (concerning the maximum admissible content of cadmium in fertilisers and the prohibition of marketing fertilisers containing higher cadmium concentrations than nationally fixed in Austria, Finland and Sweden).

The Commission, in 2001, in its decision of 13 July 2001, rejected the new draft German national provisions regarding the use of organo-stannic compounds in antifouling products. In its decision of 18 July 2001, the Commission rejected the maintenance of the German national provisions on reporting obligations with regard to adverse reactions of medicinal products.

Having extended the examination period through its decision of 13 July 2001, the Commission approved the Netherlands national provisions relating to the placing on the market and use of creosote-treated wood by its decision of 23 January 2002. Consequently, in accordance with Article 95(7) of the Treaty, the Commission is already examining the appropriateness to adapt to technical progress, for a second time, the provisions of Directive 94/60/EC regarding creosote and creosote-treated wood on the basis of the scientific evidence provided by the Netherlands and the opinion of the CSTEE given in the matter.

Finally, in its decision of 25 January 2002, the Commission declared the UK notification for maintaining the measures in the HIV testing kits and services regulations 1992, with reference to Article 95(4) of the Treaty, inadmissible. The Commission is in the process of preparing its decisions on the Austrian, Finnish and Swedish notifications with regard to cadmium contents in fertilisers.

1.5. Application of international agreements adopted by the Community and of the law derived from such agreements

Pursuant to Article 300(7) of the Treaty, agreements concluded under the conditions set out in this article are binding on the institutions of the Community and on Member States. Within that context, the Commission began proceedings against Ireland in 1998 for infringing Article 5 of Protocol 28 of the Agreement on the European Economic Area. In violation of that article, Ireland has failed to approve the Berne Convention for the Protection of Literary and Artistic Works as amended by the Paris Act (1971). The Commission referred the matter to the Court of Justice on 19 January 2000 and, in a judgment given on 19 March 2002, the Court concluded that Ireland had failed to meet its obligations resulting from the combined provisions of Article 300(7) EC and Article 5 of Protocol 28 annexed to the Agreement on the European Economic Area. It should be noted that Mr Advocate-General Mischko also rejected the United Kingdom's argument concerning the potential impact of the mixed nature of an agreement on the Commission's powers in respect of infringement proceedings.

Complaints were also lodged with the Commission concerning the failure by the United Kingdom and the Netherlands to comply with certain provisions relating to freedom of establishment and freedom of movement for workers contained in the European Agreement with Poland.

1.6. Graphical overview of all the infringement proceedings commenced or handled by the Commission during 2001

The three tables below show the numbers of infringement proceedings in motion on 31 December 2001, at the three separate stages: letter of formal notice, reasoned opinion and referral to the Court of Justice.

Cases in motion on 31 December 2001 in which infringement proceedings were commenced, by Member State

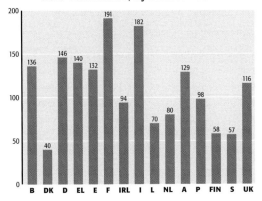

Cases in motion on 31 December 2001 for which a reasoned opinion was sent, by Member State

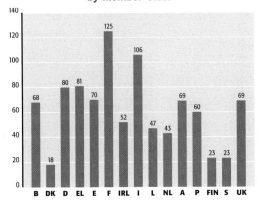

Referrals in motion on 31 December 2001, by Member State

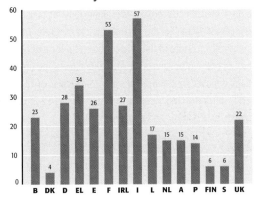

1.7. Application by the Commission of Article 228 of the EC Treaty (developments in 2000)

In 2001 the Commission explained the method whereby it calculated the amount of penalty payments proposed to the Court within the framework of referrals pursuant to Article 228 EC. This method is set out in two Commission notices of 1996 ([1]) and 1997 ([2]). In 2001 the Commission clarified how it proceeds in fixing the length of the infringement (from the date of the first Court judgment) at 0.1 point per month of delay as from the seventh month of the judgment's being delivered, within the limits laid down by its 1997 notice.

The Commission also adopted three second referral decisions with demands for penalty payments from Spain, France and Luxembourg.

The fields covered by these decisions were very diverse: one concerned the environment (Spain), one fisheries (France) and one transport (Luxembourg).

The diversity of areas concerned shows that the second referral procedure with penalty payments is no longer, as it once was, mainly limited to the environmental and social fields and therefore covers the whole range of infringements.

It should also be noted that the second referral decision against France is the first in the fisheries field.

Several files were also wound up in 2001 after the Member States concerned had taken steps to comply with the Court judgment. One such example was the file on the Kouroupitos rubbish tip, the only case to date in which the Court has required a Member State to make penalty payments. Given that measures to implement the first Court judgment were adopted by the Greek authorities on 26

([1]) Information from the Commission — memorandum on applying Article 171 of the EC Treaty, OJ C 242, 21.8.1996 p. 6.

([2]) Information from the Commission — method of calculating the penalty payments provided for pursuant to Article 171 of the EC Treaty, OJ C 63, 28.2.1997 p. 2.

February 2001, the latter paid a total of EUR 5 400 000 in penalty payments for the period from July 2000 to March 2001. This case concerned Greece's failure to take the necessary measures to ensure the elimination of toxic and dangerous waste in the Chania region of Crete (more specifically, closure of the illegal rubbish tip located at the mouth of the river Kouroupitos), in violation of the obligations imposed by Council Directive 75/442/EEC of 15 July 1975 on waste and Council Directive 78/319/EEC of 20 March 1978 on toxic and dangerous waste.

In 2001 the Commission also closed previous cases for which a solution designed to ensure compliance with the Court judgment was provided by the Member State concerned.

No file in which a second referral decision was taken in 2000 or previously is still pending.

The summary table below lists the decisions taken by the Commission for second referrals since the procedure was introduced by the Maastricht Treaty (and the outcome in each case).

Member State	Subject matter	Year/No	Initial judgment (226/EC)	Proposed penalty (EUR per day)	Date of Commission decision	Status
B	Wild birds	1990/0291	08/07/1987	7 750	10/12/1997	terminated
	Financing of students (nationality)	1989/0457	03/05/1994	43 400	22/12/1999	terminated
DE	Surface water	1987/0372	17/10/1991	158 400	29/01/1997	terminated
	Wild birds	1986/0222	03/07/1990	26 400	29/01/1997	terminated
	Groundwater	1986/0121	28/02/1991	264 000	29/01/1997	terminated
	Impact directive	1990/4710	22/10/1998	237 600	21/12/2000	case dropped
E	Directive 76/160/EC – Quality of bathing water	1989/0418	12/02/1998	45 600	23/05/2001	in motion
EL	Private schools (nationality)	1989/0165	15/03/1988	61 500	10/12/1997	terminated
	Certificates of higher education	1991/0668	23/03/1995	41 000	10/12/1997	terminated
	Public service contracts	1993/0711	02/05/1996	39 975	24/06/1998	terminated
	Kouroupitos waste dump	1989/0138	07/04/1992	24 600 judgment of 4.7.2000 = 20 000	26/06/1997	terminated
	Access to public service jobs	1991/0583	02/07/1996	57 400	01/07/1999	terminated
F	Fisheries – failure to monitor compliance with technical conservation measures	1984/0445	11/06/1991	316 500	20/12/2001	in motion
	Defective products	1989/0146	13/01/1993	158 250	31/03/1998	terminated
	Wild birds	1984/0121	27/04/1988	105 500	24/06/1998	terminated
	Night work (women)	1990/2109	13/03/1997	142 425	21/04/1999	case dropped
I	Radiation protection	1990/0240	09/06/1993	159 300	29/01/1997	terminated
	Waste management plan	1988/0239	13/012/1991	123 900	29/01/1997	terminated
	Urban waste water	1993/0786	12/12/1996	185 850	02/12/1998	terminated
	Safety at sea; prevention of pollution and living and working on board vessels	1996/0997	11/11/1999	88 500	21/12/2000	terminated
L	Access to public service jobs	1991/0222	02/07/1996	14 000	02/12/1998	terminated
	Medical assistance on board vessels	1995/0142	29/10/1998	6 000	22/12/1999	terminated
	Investigation of civil aviation accidents and incidents	1997/0107	16/12/1999	9 000	20/12/2001	in motion
UK	Quality of bathing waters (Blackpool & Southport)	1986/0214	14/07/1993	106 800	21/12/2000	case dropped

2. SITUATION SECTOR BY SECTOR

2.1. ECONOMIC AND FINANCIAL AFFAIRS

Free movement of capital

Broadly speaking, freedom of capital movements is satisfactorily secured both within the European Community and in relation to non-member countries. The number of infringement cases pending fell slightly during the report period, although some of them concern substantial barriers to the smooth operation of the single market and are at an advanced stage in the procedure.

The Court gave only one judgment in the field of the free movement of capital, finding that a national rule requiring a mortgage securing a debt payable in the currency of another Member State to be registered in the national currency was incompatible with Community law ([3]).

A fair number of the significant infringement proceedings concern the special rights enjoyed by Member States to control firms in the public utilities sector (energy, telecoms, etc.), and the issues involved are crucially important from the standpoint of integration of the single market. Following the first judgment ([4]) handed down by the Court in this area, three other similar infringement proceedings were brought, on which the Advocate General delivered his opinion ([5]) on 3 July. The Court's judgment will make it possible to fine-tune the interpretation given to the freedom to invest within the Community and determine what action should be taken with regard to other similar cases which are at a less advanced stage in the procedure.

Proceedings are continuing against a number of restrictions on the acquisition of real property by non-residents in certain Member States. These infringements, which show that the Community real-estate market is still relatively fragmented, seriously limit the exercise of fundamental freedoms by EU citizens. Other cases are still pending against restrictions on the investment activities of supplementary pension funds.

The rules applied by one Member State concerning the reporting of cross-border payments, and in particular the proportionality of the fines for non-compliance with this administrative obligation, are also the subject of infringement proceedings in which it was decided to refer the matter to the Court of Justice.

2.2. BUSINESSES

Overview

As at the end of the report period, the Enterprise DG was responsible for managing 470 directives, of which 452 were in force at that date. Complaints and infringements relating to those directives accounted for nearly 4 % of the total number of infringements dealt with by the Commission during the year; the Enterprise DG noted a decrease in its caseload in comparison with the previous year.

This is chiefly due to the fact that Member States transposed a large number of directives in respect of which infringement proceedings for failure to transpose had been initiated.

Although there were fewer infringement cases, failure to transpose directives continues to be a major problem for both businesses in the sectors concerned (namely motor vehicles, chemicals and capital goods) and consumers of the goods produced, who are unable to take full advantage of the single market. The transposal rate currently varies between 95.19 and 99.12 % according to the Member State. Most infringement proceedings for failure to transpose concern the motor-vehicle sector, followed by the chemical industry. There is no doubt that full transposal of Community law in the industrial field would enable the single market to function more smoothly.

The difficulties encountered in transposing directives can often be ascribed to the fact that the officials responsible for negotiating them are not the same as those in charge of drafting the national transposal measures and subsequently ensuring that they are applied in practice.

An increase in instances of incorrect application and faulty transposal was furthermore noted. Most of these cases concerned capital goods.

The Enterprise DG reacted to this development by systematically entering cases of incorrect application and faulty transposal on the agenda for package meetings organised by the Secretariat-General concerning the transposal of directives.

In statistical terms, it is worth noting that infringement proceedings were opened in 80 % of the cases examined by the Enterprise DG, the same high proportion as in 2000. The rate of referral to the Court also remained constant at 8 % of the total number of cases examined.

[3] Case C-464/98 — 'National rules prohibiting the registration of mortgages in foreign currencies' — judgment given on 11 January 2001.

[4] Case C-58/99 – 'Privatisation of public undertakings — grant of special powers' — judgment given on 23 May 2000.

[5] Cases C-367/98, C-483/99 and C-503/99 — 'Privatisation of strategic undertakings – restrictions on shareholding and involvement in management — specific holdings and powers of the State' — opinion delivered on 3 July 2001.

Analysis by sector

2.2.1. Chemicals

Cases of failure to transpose directives in the chemicals sector fell markedly during the year: proceedings were terminated in 23 cases, 17 of which related to directives whose transposal deadline expired in 2000. However, since there is only one directive with a transposal deadline that expired in 2001, it is too early to conclude that a trend is emerging towards a high transposal rate within a reasonable timescale. This catching-up process appears to confirm that the main reason for the failure to report measures is that the procedures for transposing directives into national law have lagged behind schedule, rather than other factors.

The only case of non-transposal that cannot apparently be ascribed to delays in the transposal process relates to explosives (Directive 93/15/EEC). This case is currently being examined under the procedure laid down in Article 228 of the Treaty following the judgment delivered by the Court in March 2000 finding that France had failed to fulfil its obligation to transpose the directive (Case C-327/98). It would nevertheless appear that transposal measures are in the process of being adopted.

As concerns faulty transposal or incorrect application, two new infringement cases were opened. These relate to the infringement of certain directives laying down restrictions on the marketing and use of dangerous substances (oil lamps, arsenic compounds) or rules on the labelling of dangerous preparations.

Two cases of faulty transposal or incorrect application concern Directive 93/15/EC on the placing on the market and supervision of explosives for civil use and involve France and Germany. In the case of Germany, the Commission decided on 23 October to refer the matter to the Court.

2.2.2. Pharmaceuticals

All proceedings for failure to transpose directives in the pharmaceuticals sector were terminated during the year. Nevertheless, problems remain with the interpretation and application of the pharmaceuticals directives by the national authorities, particularly in the case of the 'transparency' directive (Directive 89/105/EEC relating to the transparency of measures regulating the prices of medicinal products for human use and their inclusion in the scope of national health insurance systems). The directive offers procedural guarantees, together with precise deadlines, with regard to the setting of prices and the level of reimbursement of medicinal products.

Many of the Member States do not comply with the directive's requirements, with special reference to the deadlines for adopting and notifying decisions on prices of medicinal products, the obligation to give reasons for decisions taken that are based on objective and verifiable criteria, the availability of remedies for contesting decisions taken, or the conditions in which positive lists of medicinal products covered by the national health insurance system are drawn up. Among the proceedings initiated against Member States for infringement of Directive 89/105/EEC, it is worth mentioning the judgment delivered by the Court on 27 November against Austria, while a case against Finland is also before the Court. It was also decided to refer the case against Belgium to the Court, whereas the referral decision concerning Greece is currently suspended in view of discussions in progress between the Commission and the Greek authorities. Intensive discussions are also ongoing with other Member States on the subject of application of this directive.

Apart from application of the transparency directive, two major proceedings against Belgium and Italy are still ongoing. The cases relate to the application of Directive 89/381/EEC on medicinal products derived from human blood or human plasma and the conditions for suspending marketing authorisations for medicinal products in Italy. In both cases the Commission addressed a supplementary reasoned opinion to the Member State concerned.

2.2.3. Cosmetics

The Commission observed real progress during the year in the transposal of Community rules on cosmetics and was able to terminate a large number of infringement proceedings against Member States for failure to notify national measures transposing directives. All Member States have notified national measures implementing Directives 2000/6/EC and 2000/11/EC adapting to technical progress Directive 76/768/EEC and only a few Member States have not yet transposed Directives 97/18/EC and 2000/41/EC postponing the date from which experiments on animals are prohibited for ingredients or combinations of ingredients.

It also observed some progress in the application of Community rules on cosmetics, having had to handle no new infringement cases.

2.2.4. Capital goods

In the mechanical and electrical engineering sectors (including personal protection equipment), given that the latest directive to be adopted dates from 1999 (Directive 1999/5/EC on radio equipment and telecommunications terminal equipment and the mutual recognition of their conformity), few cases of failure to transpose remain. The situation regarding Directive 1999/5/EC is as follows.

France, Germany, Ireland and Italy have now transposed the directive into their national law, enabling the infringement proceedings against them to be terminated, and only Greece has not yet done so. The Commission brought an action against Greece before the Court of Justice on 18 July for failure to transpose the directive.

Major progress was achieved in remedying instances of incorrect application or faulty transposal of directives: over 60 % of infringement proceedings pending in this area were terminated during the year. A combination of frequent direct contacts with the officials responsible for the issues involved in the national administrations and strict application of the remedies available to the Commission under Article 226 of the EC Treaty yielded satisfactory results. In the area of market surveillance in particular, Member States acted more effectively than in the past and carried out the necessary checks.

In the field of measuring instruments, outstanding infringements usually relate only to failure to transpose directives; as regards pressure vessels and medical devices, most of the infringements involve incorrect application of the directives.

And in the case of gas appliances, the infringement proceedings pending relate exclusively to incorrect application of Directive 90/396/EEC on appliances burning gaseous fuels.

Regarding cases of failure to notify national transposal measures, the situation is as follows.

– It was decided on 20 December to refer Germany's failure to transpose Directive 97/23/EC on pressure vessels to the Court of Justice.

– For Directive 98/79/EC on in vitro diagnostic medical devices, all the Member States have notified national transposal measures except for France, which should complete its transposition in 2002.

– It was decided to send Greece and Portugal a reasoned opinion on account of their failure to transpose Directive 1999/103/EC on units of measurement.

Member States did not usually encounter particular problems in transposing the above three directives into national law; delays in transposal appear to have been caused, at least partly, by the complexity of their procedures.

As regards cases where national law conflicts with the directives, the situation is as follows.

– A letter of formal notice under Article 228 was sent to Italy concerning the non-conformity of its national rules with Directive 90/396/EEC on appliances burning gaseous fuels in the wake of the judgment delivered by

the Court in 1999 finding that Italy's rules were incompatible with Community law (Case C-97/112).

– A letter of formal notice was addressed to Portugal concerning non-conformity of national legislation with Directive 93/42/EEC on medical devices.

2.2.5. Motor vehicles, tractors and motorcycles

A satisfactory pace has been reached in the transposal of directives governing the type-approval of motor vehicles, agricultural or forestry tractors and motorcycles. A major reason for this appears to be that, in contrast to the previous year, 2001 witnessed a smaller number of directives (11) reaching transposition deadlines. This resulted in a markedly lower legislative burden in the Member States. The initiation of infringement proceedings is generally sufficient to secure the transposition of directives within a reasonable deadline, obviating the need for further action in the Court of Justice.

Nonetheless it is to be noted that on 15 March the Court delivered a judgment in Case C-83/00 declaring that, by failing to adapt its laws, regulations and administrative measures in order to fulfil the requirements of Directive 97/24/EC on certain components and characteristics of two or three-wheel motor vehicles, the Netherlands had failed to comply with its obligations under the EC Treaty.

Thanks to the adoption of road traffic amending legislation in Austria, a number of infringement cases arising from that Member State's failure to transpose directives on time can now be closed.

Owing both to the complexity of legislation and to constantly evolving technology, the type-approval of vehicles gives rise to frequent difficulties in interpretation. The Commission notes with satisfaction that the type-approval authorities themselves make frequent recourse to well-established mutual information and discussion networks in order to resolve potential difficulties in the application of the legislative provisions. The Commission works closely with Member States in order to identify those instances where the legislative framework is in possible need of amendment.

2.2.6. Preventive rules provided for by Directive 98/34/EC

The Enterprise DG is also responsible for administering Directive 98/34/EC. The directive establishes a notification procedure which requires Member States to submit to the Commission, and to each other, their drafts of new technical regulations for monitoring of compliance with internal market rules before they are finally adopted. The notification procedure is an essential tool for preventing barriers to trade being created and for sharing information.

During the year the Commission received 530 drafts of technical regulations (of which 25 relating to rules on information society services and the rest relating to products) which were scrutinised by the relevant departments. These were fewer than in 2000, chiefly as a result of the drop in the number of notifications in the telecommunications sector: Directive 1999/5/EC on radio equipment and telecommunications terminal equipment, which had to be transposed by April 2000, required Member States to notify their radio interfaces, something which they did mainly in 2000. Nevertheless, there was a slight increase in the number of cases which prompted the Commission to issue a detailed opinion recommending changes to the planned measure in order to eliminate any unjustified barriers to the free movement of goods or information-society services which might arise as a result. This shows that, although the number of draft technical regulations fell, their complexity and the barriers to free movement which they are liable to create was on the increase. Alongside infringements of the EC Treaty a large proportion of the detailed opinions issued by the Commission pointed out that the projects notified could breach Community directives connected with the free movement of information-society products or services. In 15 or so cases the directive also helped to facilitate Community harmonisation by precluding the adoption of national measures that could have entrenched the positions of certain Member States when common solutions were being sought. Most of these cases concerned matters covered by the proposal for a directive on measuring instruments (COM(2000) 566 final) and the proposal for a directive on the animal-health requirements applicable to non-commercial movement of pet animals (COM(2000) 529 final).

When the Commission discovers a breach of Directive 98/34/EC, either because a legislative instrument containing technical regulations has been adopted without being notified under the directive, or because the standstill periods provided for by the directive have not been complied with, it starts a dialogue with the Member State concerned in order to see that the situation is rectified (e.g. through the notification of a new draft) or commences infringement proceedings. At the end of the year preparatory work was under way on around 15 procedures of this type, notably in the field of information-society services, which have also been subject to the notification procedure since 5 August 1999. The increase in the number of infringements in the information-society services field is due to the fact that this is a new and complex sector in which the Member States

are still having difficulty ensuring that Directive 98/34/EC is correctly applied.

In its judgment of 15 February in Case C-230/99 *Commission v France*, the Court of Justice spelled out the relationship between detailed opinions issued under Directive 98/34/EC and letters of formal notice sent to Member States pursuant to Article 226 of the EC Treaty as part of infringement proceedings. The Court held that a detailed opinion under Directive 83/189/EEC (consolidated by Directive 98/34/EC) could not be regarded as equivalent to a letter of formal notice since, when it was issued, the Member State to which it is addressed could not have committed an infringement of Community law as the instrument in question existed only in draft form.

To improve the dialogue with firms, projects notified are accessible at

http://europa.eu.int/comm/enterprise/tris/index_en.htm.

2.2.7. Other sectors

In the other sectors for which the Enterprise DG is responsible (such as textiles, toys, construction, tourism, etc.) very few infringements were observed. The following three cases are to be mentioned.

– The Commission sent Belgium a letter of formal notice for incorrect application of Directive 94/25/EC on recreational craft.

– The last set of infringement proceedings still ongoing in the construction sector regarding quality controls on certain steel imports into Greece was terminated following the adoption by the Greek authorities of a ministerial decision amending the legislation at issue.

– It was decided to refer to the Court the case against Italy concerning concessions on entrance fees for Italian museums and monuments applicable only to Italian nationals.

2.3. COMPETITION

In 2001 the Commission took decisions on 36 cases dealt with by the Directorate-General for Competition ([6]). In 32 of them the case was closed and in the remaining ones it was decided to bring the defaulting Member State before the Court of Justice. Although it is hard to draw any wide-ranging conclusions from these figures, it is safe to state that in general, Member States take steps to comply with EC competition law. Indeed, competition cases represent no more than a small fraction of the alleged infringements of EC law by Member States which the Commission is currently examining. Most of the complaints lodged with the Commission appear unfounded, do not take priority as they have no Community dimension or can be dismissed because they are being dealt with appropriately by the Member State concerned at the time the Commission makes its assessment. A large proportion of the infringement cases examined by the Directorate-General for Competition relate to the enforcement of competition directives in the telecommunications field or on the transparency of financial relations between Member States and their public undertakings. Finally, there is a growing number of cases concerning services of general interest, where the Commission needs to ensure that restrictions of competition do not exceed what is necessary to guarantee the effective performance of the tasks assigned to the service operators.

2.3.1. Telecommunications

The Commission continued to monitor the effective implementation in the Member States of directives in the competition field based on Article 86(3) of the EC Treaty, as well as establishment of the regulatory framework in Greece following the full liberalisation of telecommunications markets which took effect from 1 January. It pressed ahead with proceedings under Article 226 already initiated against certain Member States.

It also examined closely effective application of the directives in conjunction with the Member States and other interested parties as part of the preparation of the seventh report, adopted on 28 November, on the implementation of the telecommunications regulatory package ([7]).

At the end of the year 20 infringement proceedings were still ongoing against Member States that had failed to transpose the directives correctly or to notify any transposal measures, and proceedings were terminated in six cases.

The Commission pressed ahead in particular with proceedings against Luxembourg concerning rights of way and brought an action against that Member State before the Court of Justice in February for having failed to adopt clear-cut rules ensuring non-discriminatory treatment of operators with regard to rights of way.

On 16 October the Court of Justice held in the Commission's favour in the proceedings it had brought against Portugal and Greece. In the judgment concerning Portugal (Case C-429/99) the Court confirmed that callback services did not constitute voice telephony within the meaning of Directive 90/388/EEC and that the Portuguese Government was therefore wrong to reserve them for the incumbent operator pending telecoms liberalisation. In the judgment concerning Greece (Joined Cases C-396/99 and C-397/99) the Court confirmed that in accordance with

Directive 90/388/EEC access to the telecommunications market could be restricted only on the grounds of a lack of available frequencies. Where access was conditional on obtaining a licence, the Member State had to ensure that the procedures for obtaining a licence were transparent and made public and that they were applied on the basis of objective criteria and in a non-discriminatory manner.

On 6 December the Court ruled in a dispute between the Commission and France concerning the arrangements for financing the universal service in force in that country since 1997. The Commission had referred the dispute to the Court in April 2000. The Court upheld the Commission's view entirely, finding that the French arrangements did not comply with the principles of proportionality, objectivity and transparency required by the directives and that France had also failed to fulfil its obligations as regards tariff rebalancing.

Again on the issue of the tariff rebalancing required by Directive 96/19/EC, the Commission moved forward in the infringement proceedings against Spain by sending it a supplementary reasoned opinion in July. This document laid particular emphasis on the inconsistency between the completely unbundled tariffs for access to the local loop, set in December 2000, and the price cap scheme adjusted in May 2001, which continued to risk causing a cost/price squeeze until 2003, thereby undermining the results of unbundling. The measures announced by the Spanish authorities in their response to the supplementary reasoned opinion were unsatisfactory and the Commission accordingly referred the matter to the Court of Justice on 21 December.

In July a reasoned opinion was issued to Italy for failure to communicate before the prescribed deadline its measures transposing Directive 1999/64/EC on cable television networks. No reaction to its reasoned opinion having been received, the Commission decided on 20 December to refer Italy to the Court.

2.3.2. Postal services

In the postal sector, on 23 October the Commission adopted a decision under Article 86(3) of the EC Treaty on scrutiny of the relations between the French postal operator La Poste and firms specialised in providing mail preparation services. The Commission found that La Poste faced a conflict of interests in its relations with private mail preparation firms in that it was both a competitor and, on account of its postal monopoly, an unavoidable partner for such firms. The Commission took the view that this conflict of interest encouraged La Poste to abuse its dominant position. As French law did not provide for sufficiently effective or inde-

([7]) COM(2001) 706 final.

pendent scrutiny to neutralise this conflict of interest, the Commission concluded that France had infringed Article 86 read in conjunction with Article 82 of the EC Treaty.

2.3.3. State aid

The Commission examined the transposal of Directive 2000/52/EC ([8]) by Member States and opened infringement proceedings against all of them for failure to communicate such measures within the deadline laid down by the directive. On 20 December it was able to drop the proceedings against Austria, Denmark, Germany and the United Kingdom following the notification of such measures.

2.4. EMPLOYMENT AND SOCIAL AFFAIRS

The cases for which the Directorate-General for Employment and Social Affairs is responsible relate to a range of different fields (free movement of workers, equal treatment of men and women, working conditions and health and safety at work) and legal instruments (the Treaty, regulations and directives). The following general remarks can be made: in the field of the freedom of movement for workers, the problems encountered are above all specific issues relating to the incorrect application of certain Treaty provisions and regulations, whereas in other areas (equal treatment of men and women, working conditions and health and safety at work) problems have to do mainly with the non-conformity, and occasionally the failure to communicate, national measures transposing directives.

Analysis of experience in dealing with infringements nevertheless reveals that their causes and origins are varied. The role of the social partners, who participate fully in the preparation and implementation of social legislation, is also worth mentioning in this context. There would therefore seem to be no 'one size fits all' solution, and a case-by-case approach is called for.

The most significant individual cases are outlined below.

In the field of the free movement of persons, problems remain here and there owing to incorrect application of the relevant provisions of the Treaty and Regulations (EEC) Nos 1408/71 and 1612/68. A large number of proceedings already opened were continued. One example is the difficulty of obtaining recognition of work experience in the public service in several Member States (a reasoned opinion was sent to Belgium, France and Germany, while the case against Austria is continuing and it was decided to refer Ireland to the Court of Justice). The cases against France concerning the deduction of the 'contribution

sociale généralisée' and the 'contribution pour le remboursement de la dette sociale' from the income of frontier workers are being pursued under Article 228 of the Treaty following the judgments delivered by the Court ([9]). Although steps have since been taken to comply with the Court's judgments, there are still practical problems to do with the reimbursement arrangements and limitation periods which have prevented the cases being closed. Italy having failed to communicate any national measures taken in order to comply with the Court's ruling ([10]) against that Member State for non-recognition of the acquired rights of former foreign-language assistants by certain Italian universities, the proceedings in question are also continuing under Article 228 of the Treaty. On the other hand, infringement proceedings against Belgium ([11]) concerning reimbursement of university registration fees unduly charged to students from other Member States, which were being continued under Article 228, were closed following positive developments.

As regards equal treatment of men and women, the proceedings against France under Article 228 of the Treaty concerning the ban on night work for women in industry were finally terminated following the adoption of national measures lifting the ban. France also having communicated national measures transposing Directive 96/97/EC ([12]) and complied with the Court's judgment ([13]), the proceedings still ongoing against it under Article 228 were closed. Proceedings against Greece for failure to comply with the Court's judgment finding that it had failed to communicate measures transposing the same directive ([14]) are continuing, however.

The case against Greece for incorrect application of Directives 75/117/EEC and 79/7/EEC (failure to repeal, with retroactive effect, provisions of collective agreements making the payment of family and marriage allowances to female workers subject to conditions not required of married male workers) ([15]) is also being pursued under Article 228 of the Treaty.

A reasoned opinion was addressed to the UK authorities concerning faulty transposal of Directive 96/34/EC on parental leave ([16]).

On working conditions, there are still problems to do with the non-conformity of measures transposing Directive 77/187/EEC ([17]) in Italy (where it does not apply in certain crisis situations, such as a court-approved composition with creditors or the special administration procedure) and it was decided to refer the matter to the Court. Proceedings against France were dropped following the steps it took to comply with Court rulings against it for failure to communicate measures transposing Directives 94/33/EC ([18]) and 93/104/EC ([19]), while those against Italy for failing to com-

([8]) *Commission directive of 26 July 2000 amending Directive 80/723/EEC on the transparency of financial relations between Member States and public undertakings.*

([9]) *Judgments of 15 February 2000 in Cases C-169/98 and C-34/98.*

([10]) *Judgment of 26 June 2001 in Case C-212/99.*

([11]) *For failure to comply with the judgment of 3 May 1994 in Case C-47/93.*

([12]) *Amending Directive 86/378/EEC on the implementation of the principle of equal treatment for men and women in occupational social security schemes.*

([13]) *Judgment of 8 July 1999 in Case C-354/99.*

([14]) *Judgment of 14 December 2000 in Case C-457/98.*

([15]) *Judgment of 28 October 1999 in Case C-187/98.*

([16]) *See also the request for a preliminary ruling in Case C-243/00, still pending.*

([17]) *Relating to the safeguarding of employees' rights in the event of transfers of undertakings.*

([18]) *On the protection of young people at work. Judgment of 18 May 2000 in Case C-45/99.*

([19]) *Concerning certain aspects of the organisation of working time. Judgment of 8 June 2000 in Case C-46/99.*

ply with the Court's judgment finding that it had not communicated national measures transposing Directive 93/104/EC ([20]) are being pursued under Article 228 of the Treaty.

As regards Directive 93/104/EC (working time), a reasoned opinion was sent to Denmark, which had transposed the instrument by means of collective agreements that do not cover all workers. On the transposal of Directive 98/59/EC (collective redundancies) by Italy and Portugal, infringement proceedings for non-conformity continued and it was decided to make referrals to the Court of Justice. It was also decided to refer the problems to do with the incorrect transposal by Germany of Directive 96/71/EC ([21]) to the Court, thereby affording the latter an opportunity to rule on the interpretation of the concept of 'minimum rates of pay'.

In the field of health and safety at work, the Court's rulings against Austria for failure to communicate all the national measures transposing Directives 95/30/EC ([22]), 97/59/EC ([23]) and 97/65/EC ([24]) (on risks related to exposure to biological agents at work) reveal a serious structural problem. Most infringement proceedings nevertheless concern the non-conformity of national measures transposing the basic directives and a number of specific directives which have the same legal status but are confined to the hard core of those directives. Taking as an example transposition of the Framework Directive 89/391/EEC, proceedings for incorrect transposal are continuing against France, Spain, Sweden and the United Kingdom. A reasoned opinion was addressed to Finland and Ireland, while it was decided to refer the cases concerning Luxembourg, the Netherlands and Portugal to the Court. The Commission was able to terminate proceedings concerning transposition by Belgium after satisfactory national measures were adopted. By judgment of 15 November ([25]) the Court ruled against Italy on the grounds that it had incompletely transposed the same directive. The issue of non-conformity of the Italian measures transposing Directive 90/270/EEC (work with display screen equipment) was also referred to the Court of Justice ([26]).

2.5. AGRICULTURE

In the farm sector monitoring of the application of Community law was a two-pronged effort aimed at removing barriers to the free movement of agricultural products and ensuring effective and correct application of more specific provisions of the agricultural rules.

As far as the free movement of agricultural products is concerned, the general downward trend in conventional trade barriers – such as systematic import checks and demands for certificates – was confirmed. The monitoring effort focused on measures taken by Member States reserving the use of quality labels or descriptions for products of their own regions or countries.

In this area the Commission has traditionally been faced with a number of initiatives taken by Member States or their regional authorities with the aim of raising awareness of the quality of agricultural products and foodstuffs, *inter alia* by encouraging the creation of specific labels or descriptions. It has of course taken a favourable view of any schemes designed effectively to promote the intrinsic quality of the agricultural products or foodstuffs in question and thereby to create new outlets, improve producers' incomes and offer consumers a wider choice.

It has, however, systematically initiated infringement proceedings against quality labels or descriptions which, in breach of Article 28 of the EC Treaty as interpreted by the Court in its judgments of 12 October 1978 in Case C-13/78 *Eggers* and 7 May 1997 in Case C-321/94 *Montagne*, are reserved, in law or in fact, for national or regional products whereas such products do not display any intrinsic qualitative characteristic that is duly recognised as such. Labels or descriptions of this nature give rise to arbitrary discrimination against producers and operators from other Member States and unjustified barriers to the free movement of goods.

In this context the Commission referred to the Court the case of the German CMA label carrying the indication 'Markenqualität aus deutschen Landen', which requires at least part of the production process for agricultural products and foodstuffs to be located in Germany in order to qualify (Case C-325/00, pending); it also decided to refer France to the Court in connection with 11 regional labels ([27]), and addressed a reasoned opinion to Italy on the subject of two regional quality labels ([28]).

Regarding less traditional forms of barriers to trade, such as the repeated acts of violence committed by individuals in France against fruit and vegetable imports from other Member States, in particular from Spain, and the authorities' failure to take measures to prevent such acts, it is worth recalling the judgment given by the Court of Justice on 9 November 1997 in Case C-265/95 ([29]), where it held that 'by failing to adopt all necessary and proportionate measures in order to prevent the free movement of fruit and vegetables from being obstructed by actions by private individuals, the French Republic has failed to fulfil its obligations under Article 30 of the EC Treaty (now Article 28 EC), in conjunction with Article 5 of that Treaty (now Article 10), and under the common organisations of the markets in agricultural products'. The fact that in the most recent

([20]) Judgment of 9 March 2000 in Case C-386/98.

([21]) Concerning the posting of workers in the framework of the provision of services.

([22]) Judgment of 14 June 2001 in Case C-473/99.

([23]) Judgment of 11 October 2001 in Case C-110/00.

([24]) Judgment of 11 October 2001 in Case C-111/00.

([25]) Case C-49/00.

([26]) Case C-455/00.

([27]) In the case of France the infringement proceedings relate to the following regional quality labels: 'Normandie', 'Nord - Pas-de-Calais', 'Ardennes de France', 'Limousin', 'Languedoc-Roussillon', 'Lorraine', 'Savoie', 'Franche-Comté', 'Corse', 'Midi-Pyrénées', 'Salaisons d'Auvergne' and 'Qualité France'.

([28]) In the case of Italy the infringement proceedings relate to the regional quality labels 'Regione Siciliana-Marchio Qualità' and 'Abruzzo Qualità'.

([29]) (1997) ECR I-6959.

marketing years movements of imported fruit and vegetables, notably from Spain, went unhindered suggests that the measures taken by the French Government to comply with the Court's judgment were more effective than before. A major incident nevertheless occurred during the report period, when beef producers attacked a processing plant using meat from other Member States.

In monitoring the application of specific market organisation mechanisms, the Commission continued to keep a close watch on the use of production control mechanisms and the integrated management and control system for certain Community aid schemes.

In the milk sector infringement proceedings focused on deficiencies in implementation of the milk quotas scheme and in particular the failure of the Italian and Spanish authorities fully to implement it, with special reference to their delay in definitively passing on the supplementary levy to the producers responsible for the excesses.

In the case of Italy, the proceeding initially concerned that Member State's failure to ensure that the supplementary levy deducted by purchasers where producers' individual quotas were exceeded during the 1995/96 and 1996/97 marketing years was paid to the competent authority.

The Italian authorities had taken the view that amounts collected by buyers could not be paid to the competent authority until there had been an in-depth inquiry into the level of the individual reference quantity for each producer and the level of their actual production. A commission of inquiry had revealed suspicions of major irregularities in this area, to such an extent that the very existence of excess production was called into question. The Commission closely followed the inquiries conducted by the Italian authorities and itself carried out several on-the-spot inspection visits. The work involved redetermining each individual quota and production, again cross-checking deliveries during each period on that basis and issuing a fresh notification of the amount of levy due. It was informed of the reasons for certain delays in the procedures, due in particular to the need to consult the Council of State on some of the arrangements. When it became apparent that, despite the closure of these operations with a new notification of the amount of levy due, the amounts (other than those whose immediate recovery was prevented by court rulings suspending the payment orders, representing between one and two thirds of the total depending on the period concerned), the Commission decided to continue with the proceedings and to extend them to cover periods up to 1999/2000.

A supplementary reasoned opinion was issued in December. General permission to pay in instalments,

which was also the subject of these proceedings, was recently withdrawn.

In Spain, only a fraction of the levy payable for 1993/94, 1995/96 and 1996/97 was actually paid by producers. Both producers and purchasers brought large-scale actions against decisions affecting them.

Following commencement of infringement proceedings, the Spanish authorities adopted new measures for managing the scheme, aimed in particular at avoiding large-scale recourse to the courts in the future. The key elements consisted of a compulsory scheme for collecting advance payments from producers who exceed their quota during the period and the imposition of restrictive conditions governing the approval of purchasers. The scheme's management since 1998/99 has not produced the widespread problems that were encountered in previous years.

Regarding actions commenced earlier, the Spanish authorities caused sureties to be established for the sums in dispute in the numerous cases where this had not already been done. They now consider that the levy still due is fully covered, either by these sureties or by compulsory recovery orders.

The delay by the Greek authorities, owing to internal administrative difficulties, in implementing the integrated management and control system for certain Community aid schemes under Regulation (EEC) No 3508/92 prompted the Commission to refer the matter to the Court of Justice. The regulation is aimed at harmonising and rationalising administration and control measures for certain Community aid schemes, in particular for arable farming and meat production (beef and veal, sheepmeat and goat's meat) to boost efficiency and profitability by means of a policy of preventing and punishing irregularities in EAGGF-financed operations. Article 2 of Regulation 3508/92 as amended requires each Member State to establish by 1 January 1997 an integrated system comprising: a computerised database, an alphanumeric identification system for agricultural parcels, an alphanumeric system for the identification and registration of animals, aid applications and an integrated control system. The Greek authorities have not fully met all these requirements, the aim of which is to ensure that payments made by Community bodies are in accordance with the regulations. The fact is that the identification and numbering of agricultural land parcels has not even been commenced and the procedure for registering and identifying animals is no more than embryonic. High-performance databases do not therefore exist.

Lastly, following the Court's judgment of 16 July 1998 in Case C-136/96 ([30]), the French authorities stopped allowing the marketing and presentation, in breach of Regulation (EEC) No 1576/89, of spirits made by adding a

([30]) *(1998) ECR I-4571.*

percentage of water to whisky and using the word 'whisky' as a generic sales description. The infringement proceeding initiated on account of this practice was closed. The Commission had addressed a reasoned opinion to France for authorising the marketing of spirits made in this way and bearing the word 'whisky' as a generic sales description. Regulation (EEC) No 1576/89 provides that whisky must have an alcoholic strength of at least 40 % and no water may be added to an alcoholic drink, to prevent the nature of the product being changed.

With regard to the transposition of directives in the agricultural sector, the Commission opened infringement proceedings against seven Member States for failing to transpose, on time, Parliament and Council Directive 1999/4/EC of 22 February 1999 relating to coffee extracts and chicory extracts. The national transposal measures have now been communicated and the Commission has been able to terminate the proceedings.

In 2001, as in previous years, the Commission received notification of a great many draft instruments pursuant to Directive 98/34/EC, which requires the Member States and EFTA countries to give notice prior to the adoption of any draft rules containing technical standards or regulations which might impede intra-Community trade.

In agriculture, 143 draft instruments notified by the Member States and the EFTA countries were scrutinised during the year in the light of Article 28 of the EC Treaty and relevant secondary legislation.

2.6. ENERGY AND TRANSPORT

A total of 230 infringement cases were handled during the year by the Directorate-General for Energy and Transport, of which 126 involved failure to communicate measures transposing directives and 104 concerned the faulty transposal of directives or incorrect application of Community law. The number of proceedings pending declined considerably, an increasing number of cases having been closed in the report period (114, of which 62 involving the non-communication of transposal measures). This is the direct result of the spectacular improvement in the rate of transposal of directives in the transport field, which rose from 88.5 % at 31 December 2000 to 94 % at 31 December 2001. Sixty two new infringement proceedings were initiated (including 48 cases of non-communication of transposal measures) and 10 complaints were investigated by the Energy and Transport DG. The Court ruled against Member States in 10 cases.

Energy

2.6.1. Internal market for electricity and natural gas

Parliament and Council Directive 96/92/EC of 19 December 1996 concerning common rules for the internal market in electricity was transposed by all the Member States. Belgium should have transposed the directive by 19 February 1999 but had not done so entirely: implementing decrees were still awaited and the Commission therefore decided to refer the matter to the Court of Justice. The infringement proceedings against France for incomplete transposal of the directive and non-conformity of its national implementing measures were closed.

Parliament and Council Directive 98/30/EC concerning common rules for the internal market in natural gas had to be transposed by 10 August 2000. France has still not done so and the Commission consequently decided to bring an action against it before the Court of Justice. The proceedings against Luxembourg and Portugal for failure to communicate transposal measures were closed. Germany has transposed only part of the directive, and infringement proceedings have been commenced accordingly: a reasoned opinion was addressed to the German authorities on 13 June.

The Commission is continuing its analysis of the conformity of national measures implementing the two directives in all the Member States.

2.6.2. Energy efficiency

All the directives implementing Directive 92/75/EEC of 22 September 1992 on the indication by labelling and standard product information of the consumption of energy and other resources by household appliances ([31]) have now been transposed by all the Member States.

The deadline for transposing Parliament and Council Directive 2000/55/EC of 18 September 2000 on energy efficiency requirements for ballasts for fluorescent lighting expired on 20 November and only four Member States have communicated transposal measures.

The infringement proceedings for incorrect application of Council Directive 93/76/EEC of 13 September 1993 to limit carbon dioxide emissions by improving energy efficiency (Save) were closed following the receipt of reports on application of the directive by Member States, except for Ireland and Luxembourg, to which reasoned opinions were addressed on 23 October.

2.6.3. Oil and gas

Council Directive 98/93/EC of 14 December 1998 amending Directive 68/414/EEC imposing an obligation on

([31]) Directives 94/2/EC, 95/12/EC, 95/13/EC, 96/60/EC, 96/89/EC, 97/17/EC, 98/11/EC and 1999/9/EC on the energy labelling of various household electrical appliances.

Member States to maintain minimum stocks of crude oil and/or petroleum products, due for transposal by 31 December 1999, has been transposed by all the Member States. Nevertheless, infringement proceedings were commenced against Greece for incorrect application of the directive and a letter of formal notice was sent to the Greek authorities on 23 October.

2.6.4. External relations in the energy field

The Commission decided on 20 December to initiate infringement proceedings by issuing a letter of formal notice to Ireland for violation of the obligation of unity in the Community's international representation within the International Energy Agency as enshrined in Article 10 of the EC Treaty.

Transport

In the field of Community transport law six new directives became due for transposal during the year, but there was a marked improvement in the transposal rate. The year-on-year figures for complaints received (10) by the Commission remained stable, although the number of infringement proceedings which the Commission referred to the Court of Justice was still high at 24 (as against 39 in 2000 and 30 in 1999), bringing to 61 the total number of cases pending that the Commission has decided to refer to the Court. There was also a large number of Court rulings against Member States not complied with (15, up from 9 in 2000). Six of these cases concerned Ireland [32].

2.6.5. Road transport

The transposal of Directive 98/76/EC, which seeks to promote the exercise of the freedom of establishment of road haulage operator in national and international transport by amending Directive 96/26/EC on admission to the occupation of road haulage operator and road passenger transport operator, is still worrying as four proceedings against Belgium, France, Luxembourg and Sweden [33] for failure to notify transposition measures were still continuing before the Court of Justice. The Court gave a ruling against Luxembourg on 13 December. The proceedings against Greece and Italy were closed during the year. The Finnish authorities notified provisions transposing Directive 96/26/EC in the Åland Islands, and the case against Finland was therefore closed.

Regarding safety in the transport of dangerous substances by road, Ireland has still not complied with the two Court rulings [34] against it given in 2000 for failure to communi-

cate national measures implementing Directives 94/55/EC and 96/86/EC on the approximation of the laws of the Member States with regard to the transport of dangerous goods by road or Directive 95/50/EC on uniform procedures for checks on the transport of dangerous goods by road. Directive 99/47/EC adapting for the second time to technical progress Directive 94/55/EC on the transport of dangerous goods by road has not been transposed by Ireland, and the Commission therefore decided to refer the matter to the Court. It should be noted, as pointed out last year, that Ireland has not transposed any of the directives on road or rail transport of dangerous goods; however, three cases could be closed in the first quarter of 2002.

In the same area, the rules on the appointment and vocational qualification of safety advisers for the transport of dangerous goods by road, rail and inland waterway (Directives 96/35/EC and 2000/18/EC) have been transposed by all Member States.

Ireland is the only Member State which has not yet transposed Directive 1999/52/EC adapting to technical progress Council Directive 96/96/EC on the approximation of the laws of the Member States relating to roadworthiness tests for motor vehicles and their trailers. The Commission decided on 20 December to bring the case before the Court of Justice.

As for road taxation, the infringement proceedings against Belgium for non-conformity of measures implementing Directive 93/89/EEC (taxes, tolls and charges) were terminated. The Court's judgment in the case against Austria regarding tolls at the Brenner pass [35] has not been fully complied with, and the Commission therefore issued a letter of formal notice under Article 228(2) on 20 December. Parliament and Council Directive 99/62/EC of 17 June 1999 on the charging of heavy goods vehicles for the use of certain infrastructures has been transposed by all the Member States except Belgium.

Concerning driving licences, the conformity of measures transposing Directive 91/439/EEC still gives serious cause for concern. Examination of national transposal measures reveals that in six Member States (Denmark, France, Germany, Greece [36], the Netherlands and Spain) there are many discrepancies in such matters as the minimum age for a vehicle category, renewal of licences for EU citizens no longer residing in the Member State of issue, criteria for test vehicles, the duration of the practical test and minimum requirements in terms of physical and mental aptitude. The procedures for automatic registration of licences belonging to drivers who move from one country to another are incompatible with the principle of mutual recognition of driving licences.

[32] Three cases involving non-compliance with a Court judgment could be definitively closed in the first quarter of 2002.

[33] The proceedings against Sweden could be closed in the first quarter of 2002.

[34] Judgment of 26 September 2000 in Case C-408/99.

Judgment of 14 December 2000 in Case C-347/99.

[35] Judgment of 26 September 2000 in Case C-205/98.

[36] The proceedings against Greece could be closed in the first quarter of 2002.

The Court's judgment of 29 January 1998 ([37]) finding against Italy for failing to comply with Decision 93/496/EEC on State aid illegally granted to road haulage firms in Italy has still not been complied with, and a reasoned opinion under Article 228 of the Treaty was therefore addressed to the Italian authorities on 11 July. This is the first time in the history of Community law that proceedings for failure to recover illegal aid have reached this stage.

2.6.6. Combined transport

The Court ruled ([38]) in proceedings against Italy for non-conformity of national measures implementing Directive 92/106/EEC on the establishment of common rules for certain types of combined transport of goods between Member States. This case could, however, be closed in the first quarter of 2002 following the adoption during the year of amending legislation by Italy.

2.6.7.   Inland waterways

The Commission started proceedings against Finland for failure to transpose five directives in the inland waterways sector ([39]) and decided on 21 December to issue reasoned opinions. Transposal of Directive 96/50/EC on harmonisation of the conditions for obtaining national boatmasters' certificates for inland waterway navigation, which was due for transposal in 1998, has given rise to non-notification proceedings. The Court of Justice ruled against France on 20 September ([40]), while the case against the Netherlands was finally closed.

Proceedings against Germany and Luxembourg, which have concluded bilateral inland waterways agreements with third countries, are continuing with the Commission's decision to refer the two cases to the Court of Justice on the grounds that this is exclusively a matter for the Community. The decision has, however, been suspended until the Court gives a ruling on pending open skies cases.

2.6.8. Rail transport

In the field of carriage of dangerous goods by rail, Directive 96/49/EC as amended by Directive 96/87/EC provides for the approximation of the laws of the Member States with regard to the transport of goods, laying down uniform safety rules in this sector to improve safety and facilitate movement of rolling stock and equipment throughout the Community. These directives, which apply to transport of dangerous goods by rail in or between Member States, have still to be transposed in Ireland, which has furthermore not complied with the Court's judgment ([41]) finding that it had failed to adopt measures transposing the two

directives. Directive 1999/48/EC adapting for the second time to technical progress Council Directive 96/49/EC on the approximation of the laws of the Member States with regard to the transport of dangerous goods by rail has not been transposed by Ireland or Italy, and the Commission has accordingly decided to refer the two cases to the Court of Justice.

Directive 1999/36/EC on transportable pressure equipment and Directive 2001/2/EC on the same topic, which were due for transposal by 1 July 2001, have not yet been transposed by Belgium, Germany, Greece, Ireland, Italy or Portugal.

The situation regarding Directive 96/48/EC on the interoperability of the trans-European high-speed rail system, the purpose of which is to promote interconnection and interoperability between national high-speed rail networks at different stages of design, construction and entry into service, but also of operation and access to networks, remains highly preoccupying despite some improvement during the year. Four Member States (Austria, Finland, Ireland and the United Kingdom) have still not notified transposal measures, and the Commission has had to refer the cases against all of them to the Court of Justice. The proceedings against France, Greece and Sweden were terminated during the year. The Court ruled against Ireland on 13 December. It should be stressed in this connection that the directive must be transposed even if there are no high-speed trains in Ireland and that it does not require technical specifications for interoperability (STIs) to be drawn up prior to transposal.

2.6.9. Air transport

The rate of transposal of air transport directives is highly satisfactory at nearly 98 %. This is chiefly due to the fact that no new directives fell due for transposal in 2000 and 2001. The rate of transposal is actually 100 % for all Member States except Ireland and Luxembourg. Ireland has still not transposed Directives 98/20/EC and 1999/28/EC on the limitation of the operation of subsonic civil aeroplanes, despite the undertakings it gave last year, and both cases were referred to the Court. Directive 94/56/EC establishing the fundamental principles governing the investigation of civil aviation accidents and incidents had not been transposed by Luxembourg, prompting the judgment given on 16 December 1999 ([42]) and the Commission's decision to bring an action before the Court under Article 228 of the Treaty.

The Commission was finally able to terminate proceedings against France for incorrect application of Directive 91/670/EEC on mutual acceptance of personnel licences for the exercise of functions in civil aviation.

([37]) *Case C-280/95.*

([38]) *Judgment of 10 May 2001 in Case C-444/99.*

([39]) *Directives 76/135/EEC, 82/714/EEC, 87/540/EEC, 91/672/EEC and 96/50/EC.*

([40]) *Case C-468/00.*

([41]) *Judgment of 20 September 2001 in Case C-370/00.*

([42]) *Case C-138/99.*

Complaints about incorrect application of Directive 96/67/EC on ground handling at airports have prompted infringement proceedings against Germany and Italy. A reasoned opinion was issued to the latter on 24 July.

The infringements noted in connection with airport taxes also continued. Imposition by Member States of varying rates of tax depending on passenger destinations (internal flights/intra-Community and/or international routes) is incompatible with the principle of freedom to provide services stipulated in the field of air transport by Regulation (EEC) No 2408/92. The Court found against Italy and Portugal [43], but those judgments were not complied with and proceedings are therefore continuing under Article 228(2) of the Treaty. The case against the Netherlands is still pending before the Court, while those against Greece and Spain were terminated.

The infringement proceedings against Belgium, Denmark, Germany, Finland, Luxembourg, Austria and Sweden relating to bilateral open-skies agreements with the United States and the proceedings against the United Kingdom relating to the Bermuda II bilateral agreement are continuing in the Court of Justice. Referral decisions were taken in the infringement proceedings against France and the Netherlands concerning the open-skies agreements.

Lastly, proceedings are still pending against Greece for incorrect application of Regulation 3922/1991 on the harmonisation of technical requirements and administrative procedures in the field of civil aviation.

2.6.10. Transport by sea

The Commission notes that there has been considerable progress in implementing Community sea transport law in the whole area of safety at sea, but the situation regarding freedom to provide services is less satisfactory. The rate of transposal rose from 88 % in 2000 to 96.9 % in 2001. No new directives fell due for transposal during the year. The Netherlands has transposed none of the directives that were adopted in 1999 and whose transposition deadline expired in 2000.

Directive 99/35/EC on a system of mandatory surveys for the safe operation of regular ro-ro ferry and high-speed passenger craft services has been transposed by all Member States [44] (except for Austria, Finland, Luxembourg, the Netherlands and Portugal) and Directive 99/97/EC on port State control has yet to be transposed in Luxembourg and the Netherlands.

Regarding the safety of passenger transport by sea, Directives 98/18/EC and 98/41/EC have finally been transposed in all Member States. Infringement proceedings against Portugal will be terminated in early 2002. These directives seek to improve safety and likelihood of rescue for passengers and crew on passenger ships bound for or leaving Community ports and to ensure more effective action in the event of an accident. However, proceedings for incorrect transposal are continuing against France and Italy, with those against Belgium still pending before the Court.

On the other hand, all the infringement proceedings for incorrect transposal of Directive 94/57/EC on common rules and standards to be observed by the Member States and ship-inspection, survey and certification organisations so as to ensure compliance with international conventions on maritime safety and marine pollution were terminated during the year.

Directive 95/21/EC (port State control), which harmonises ship inspection criteria, including rules for detention and/or refusal of access to Community ports, was finally transposed in all Member States and proceedings against Italy were terminated. Italy has also transposed the amending Directives 98/25/EC and 98/42/EC (port State control). The cases commenced against France and Ireland for incorrect application of Directive 95/21/EC requiring Member States to inspect at least 25 % of all ships flying foreign flags that land in their ports or navigate waters under their jurisdiction are continuing.

As for the human element, Luxembourg and the Netherlands have still not yet notified full measures transposing Directive 98/35/EC amending Directive 94/58/EC on the minimum level of training of seafarers. The Court of Justice ruled on 3 July against Luxembourg [45].

The transposal of Directive 97/70/EC setting up a harmonised safety regime for fishing vessels of 24 metres in length and over, as amended by Directive 1999/19/EC, is still creating numerous difficulties in the Netherlands, which has not yet transposed the two directives, and both cases are before the Court. Proceedings against Belgium for failure to notify measures transposing the amending directive will be terminated in early 2002. Proceedings are still in motion against Italy for non-conformity.

Compliance with Community legislation on registration and flag rights continues to be a problem. Arrangements for entering vessels in shipping registers and granting flag rights remain discriminatory in the Netherlands, against which proceedings are continuing before the Court.

As regards right of establishment, the Commission has decided to refer to the Court the case against Italy for non-conformity with Articles 43 and 48 of the Treaty of its national legislation specifying the conditions on which shipping lines lawfully established in another Member State may participate on the same terms as Italian shipping lines in the Italian conference traffic quota.

As regards maritime cabotage, proceedings are in hand

[43] *Judgments of 4 and 26 July 2001 in Cases C-447/99 and C-70/99 respectively.*

[44] *The proceedings against Sweden will be terminated in early 2002.*

[45] *Case C-297/00.*

against several Member States (Denmark, Germany, Greece, Portugal and Spain) for maintaining or adopting national rules in breach of Regulation (EEC) No 3577/92, which provides for maritime cabotage to be opened up to Community shipowners operating ships registered in and flying the flag of a Member State. The case against France for incorrect transposal of the maritime cabotage rules was closed.

The principle of freedom to provide services where cargo-sharing agreements between Member States and third countries are concerned, enshrined in Regulation (EEC) No 4055/86, is not yet respected by all Member States. Proceedings initiated in 2000 against Italy are still ongoing. Proceedings are continuing against Belgium ([46]). It was reported last year that cases might be closed in 2001, but protocols with the relevant non-member countries have not yet entered into force and the procedure is therefore moving forward with the issue of reasoned opinions under Article 228(2) of the Treaty. The case concerning the cargo-sharing agreement between Portugal and Yugoslavia ([47]) is still being pursued, although it might be closed in the first half of 2002. The case concerning Angola was closed.

The Commission also pays special attention to the application of Regulation (EEC) No 4055/86, given the possible forms of discrimination on grounds of nationality between operators and types of transport and the barriers they can raise. Two infringement proceedings are in motion concerning the discriminatory dock dues imposed in Greece and Italy. The dues vary in accordance with the port of destination: the amounts are lower for shipping between two ports in national territory than for international shipping. The case against Italy is currently before the Court of Justice. Several similar cases involving other Member States are under scrutiny.

Lastly, infringement proceedings against Finland were commenced (and will be opened formally in early 2002) for failing to take the necessary steps to prevent blockades of Finnish ports against certain ships from non-member countries.

2.7. INFORMATION SOCIETY

The Lisbon European Council was a key stage in the convergence of the European electronic communication sector. The Heads of State and Government reaffirmed their determination to see Europe evolve towards a digital, paperless economy, an intention which has since been given substance in the eEurope Action Plan. Another important event is now approaching: the adoption by

Parliament and the Council of a new regulatory framework ([48]). The aim of this is to increase competition within and convergence of, markets, and forms part of the complete, coherent implementation of the current European legislation.

As far as the transposal of the regulatory framework (13 directives, one regulation and four decisions) is concerned, the Seventh Report on the Implementation of the Telecommunications Regulatory Package ([49]) notes that, in 2001, at least three States (France, Italy and Luxembourg) had notified their new legislation to the Commission, thus responding to its main concerns. In Greece, the national legislation was consolidated following full liberalisation, thus providing greater clarity and legal certainty.

As a result, of the cases concerning failure of national implementing measures to comply with Community law or incorrect application of Community law, in 2001 a significant number was closed (13) or suspended (four) in view of the progress made by the Member States in transposing Community law. Germany is the most notable example. Proceedings had been launched pursuant to the provisions of Directive 97/13/EC on licences, because the level of fees set exceeded the level necessary to cover administrative costs. However, the German administrative courts repealed the national legislation on the level of these fees, and the action undertaken before the EC Court of Justice was consequently suspended.

In addition, six ongoing procedures for failure to transpose have been closed on the basis of the provisions set out by Directive 97/51/EC on leased lines (France and Italy), Directive 98/10/EC on voice telephony (Italy) and Article 5 of Directive 97/66/EC concerning the processing of personal data and the protection of privacy in the telecommunications sector (France, Ireland, United Kingdom). At the end of the year, following a ruling by the EC Court of Justice (case C-319/99), France also notified its implementing measures for Directive 95/47/EC on the use of standards for the transmission of television signals. However, in two cases concerning France on the one hand (C-151/00), and the Netherlands on the other (C-254/00), there has still been no notification, even though the Court of Justice noted the failure to transpose in 2001. Consequently, the Commission took steps pursuant to Article 228 of the Treaty and, on 21 December 2001, sent France a reasoned opinion.

The Court has ruled against Luxembourg (Case C-448/99) and France (Case C-146/100) in other cases for non-conformity of the national legislation with, in the first case, Directive 97/13/EC on licences and, in the second, with Directive 97/33/EC on interconnection. The second case had particu-

([46]) *Judgments of 14 September 1999 in Cases C-170/98 and C-171/98.*

([47]) *Judgments of 4 July 2000 in Cases C-62/98 and C-84/98.*

([48]) *Cf. http://europa.eu.int/information_society/topics/telecoms/new_rf/index_en.htm*

([49]) *COM(2001) 706 of 26 November 2001; the electronic version is available at: http://europa.eu.int/information_society/topics/telecoms/implementation/annual_report/7report/index_en.htm.*

lar relevance to the requirements of the universal service fund. Thus, because of the growing body of case law in the sector, the Information Society Directorate-General now publishes on its web site a 'Guide to the case law of the European Court of Justice in the field of telecommunications'([50]), which is regularly updated.

At the end of 2001, there were 69 ongoing infringement procedures, 12 of which had been opened on the basis of complaints lodged by the Directorate-General for the Information Society. There are still a considerable number of ongoing actions which have been brought for failure to notify implementing measures (14 since the entry into force of the directive on electronic signature ([51]) on 18 July 2001). Furthermore, the number of cases relating to non-conformity of Community law (19) or to the incorrect application of the latter via implementing measures (36) is constantly rising.

It should also be noted that, at the end of 2001, a significant number of infringement proceedings had been closed by a judgment by the Court of Justice (three for failure to notify, three for non-conformity, three for incorrect application) or had been the subject of a reasoned opinion (one for failure to notify, five for non-conformity and three for incorrect application).

The principal questions pending are now the following.

After proceedings were initiated in 2000 against nine Member States pursuant to Directive 98/61/EC on number portability, reasoned opinions were sent to the Netherlands and the United Kingdom, and cases were referred to the Court of Justice concerning Germany and Sweden, on the one hand, for failure to preselect an operator for local calls, and France, on the other, for lack of total portability of the number.

In 2001, in order to ensure a minimum level for the free detailed invoices provided to consumers, thus enabling them to check the cost of calls, proceedings were initiated against six Member States under the new Directive 98/10/EC on voice telephony. Reasoned opinions were sent to Luxembourg and Austria on the same subject before the end of the year.

There still remains a fairly small number of cases of incomplete transposition or failure to notify. These mainly concern Directives 97/66/EC and 95/47/EC, as referred to above.

Six infringement proceedings for failure to notify national implementing measures were opened in 2001 pursuant to the directive on electronic signatures. Letters of formal notice were therefore sent to Ireland, Italy, the Netherlands, Finland, Portugal and the United Kingdom. The European Commission also decided to open infringe-

ment proceedings against Greece, Portugal and Germany for not ensuring that shared access to the local loop was offered to competitors in conformity with the Regulation on unbundled access to the local loop ([52]), which has applied since 2 January 2001 (cf. IP/01/1896).

Overall, given the extent of the current legislation in telecommunications and the relatively short time which has elapsed since it was adopted in its entirety, there has been a remarkable degree of transposal, thanks to the efficiency of infringement proceedings (more than 200 cases have been closed in the last three years).

2.8. ENVIRONMENT

2.8.1. Introduction

The environment sector represented over a third of the complaints and infringement cases concerning instances of non-compliance with Community law investigated by the Commission in 2001. During this year, the Commission brought 71 cases against Member States before the Court of Justice and delivered 197 reasoned opinions (on the basis of either Article 226 or 228). This marks an increase of approximately 40 % on the corresponding figures of the previous year. In this respect, it must be borne in mind that the Commission aims to settle suspected infringements as soon as they are identified without it being necessary to initiate formal infringement proceedings.

The increasing number of environmental cases is due to several factors.

– The Commission's regular monitoring of the conformity of the national implementing measures notified by the Member States pursuant to their obligation to transpose Community directives.

– The public's increasing concern on environmental issues, and its greater awareness of Community environmental law and of the possibility to bring instances of non-compliance to the attention of the Commission, in particular in the framework of Commission's complaints handling ([53]).

– The organisational difficulties in the Member States in ensuring full compliance with Community environmental law, arising from their own constitutional and/or administrative structure, since responsibility for implementation often lies with more than one authority (different ministries, central, regional or local authorities, etc.).

– The wide scope and the ambition of Community environmental legislation, in particular in key directives such as Directive 92/43/EEC on the conservation of

([50]) http://europa.eu.int/ information_society/ topics/telecoms/ implementation/ infringement/doc/ guidecaselaw.pdf

([51]) Directive 1999/93/EC of the European Parliament and of the Council of 13 December 1999 on a Community framework for electronic signatures, OJ L 13, 19.1.2001, p. 12.

([52]) Regulation No 2887/2000 of the European Parliament and of the Council of 18 December 2000 on unbundled access to the local loop, OJ L 336, 30.12.2000, p. 4.

([53]) See standard form for complaints to the Commission, OJ C 119, 30.4.1999, p. 5.

natural habitats and wild flora and fauna ([54]) or Directive 85/337/EEC on the assessment of the effects of certain public and private projects on the environment ([55]), as modified by Directive 97/11/EC ([56]). Both of them include far-reaching environmental assessment obligations to be taken into account in planning and authorising a specific project and therefore involve decision-making across a wide range of policy sectors that are in many cases devolved to several regional and local authorities and attract a great deal of public attention.

— The non-existence or relative inefficiency of complaint mechanisms in Member States.

Recourse to the infringement proceedings set out in Articles 226 and 228 of the EC Treaty is not, however, the only, nor often the most efficient way to ensure compliance with environmental directives. In many cases, complainants can obtain satisfaction more quickly by using means of redress under national law. The possibility of creating cheaper and more efficient access to justice at Member State level in line with the Århus Convention ([57]), as well as the establishment of reliable national/regional complaint mechanisms and arbitration schemes, will be the subject of a proposal for a directive to be tabled in 2002.

The Commission, and in particular its Environment DG, has, in its turn, increased its efforts to take a more proactive approach towards the Member States to help them better transpose and apply environmental directives. Several seminars were held in 2001 in a number of Member States where the Commission's view on the correct implementation of particularly complex environmental directives was explained to the competent authorities with a view to preventing, rather than correcting, instances of bad application.

The Article 228 procedure has continued to serve as a last resort to force Member States to comply with the judgments given by the European Court of Justice. In 2001, the Commission brought three cases before the Court under Article 228 and sent 15 letters of formal notice and seven reasoned opinions for failure to notify, non-conformity or incorrect application under Article 228. Two of the three cases brought before the Court in 2001 under Article 228 were withdrawn as the Member States concerned took the necessary measures to comply with the judgment. More details are given in Annex V to this report.

The Commission is continuing the practice of using Article 10 of the Treaty, which requires Member States to cooperate in good faith with the Community institutions, in the event of a consistent lack of reply to Commission letters of request for information. This lack of cooperation prevents the Commission from acting effectively as guardian of the Treaty.

No major developments have occurred since last year's report on the notification by Member States of measures implementing environmental legislation. Nine directives fell due for transposition in 2001.

As before, the Commission was forced to start proceedings in several cases of failure to notify it of transposing measures. Details are given in the sections on individual sectors and directives and in Annex IV (Parts 1 and 2) of this report. Proceedings are in hand in all areas of environmental legislation and against all the Member States in connection with the conformity of national transposing measures. Monitoring the action taken to ensure conformity of Member States' legislation with the requirements of the environmental directives is a priority task for the Commission. In connection with transposition of Community provisions into matching national provisions, there has been some improvement as regards the provision, along with the statutory instruments transposing the directives, of detailed explanations and concordance tables. This is done by Germany, Finland, Sweden, the Netherlands, France and sometimes Denmark and Ireland. The Commission is also responsible for checking that Community environmental law (directives and regulations) is properly applied, and this is a major part of its work. This means checking Member States' practical steps to fulfil certain general obligations (designation of zones, production of programmes, management plans etc.) and examining specific cases in which a particular administrative practice or decision is alleged to be contrary to Community law. Complaints and petitions sent to the European Parliament by individuals and non-governmental organisations, and written and oral parliamentary questions and petitions, generally relate to incorrect application.

As stated in the previous report, the Commission must, when considering individual cases, assess factual and legal situations that are very tangible and are of direct concern to the public. It therefore encounters certain practical difficulties. Without abandoning the pursuit of incorrect application cases (especially those which highlight questions of principle or general interest or administrative practices that contravene the directives) the Commission consequently concentrates on problems of communication and conformity.

The Commission continued work in 2001 as a follow-up to the communication adopted in October 1996 (implementing Community environmental law), in particular with regard to environmental inspections. In this respect, the adoption of the recommendation of the European Parliament and the Council on minimum criteria for environmental in-

([54]) OJ L 206, 22.7.1992, p. 7.

([55]) OJ L 175, 5.7.1985, p. 40.

([56]) OJ L 73, 14.3.1997, p. 5.

([57]) UN/ECE Convention on access to information, public participation in decision-making and access to justice in environmental matters.

spections (2001/331/EC) is particularly worth noting. The recommendation draws heavily on the work which had been done in previous projects under IMPEL ('Implementation and enforcement of EU environmental law' network). It includes several tasks which IMPEL is specifically invited to undertake and it will be one of the principal features of IMPEL's work programme over the next few years. These include establishing a scheme under which Member States report and offer advice on inspectorates and inspection procedures in Member States; drawing up minimum criteria concerning the qualifications of environmental inspectors and developing training programmes; and preventing illegal cross-border environmental practices by coordinating inspections with regard to installations which might have significant cross-border impact.

2.8.2. Freedom of access to information

Directive 90/313/EEC on the freedom of access to information on the environment is a particularly important piece of general legislation: keeping the public informed ensures that all environmental problems are taken into account, encourages enlightened and effective participation in collective decision-making and strengthens democratic control. The Commission believes that, through this instrument, ordinary citizens can make a valuable contribution to protecting the environment.

Although all Member States have notified national measures transposing the directive, there are several cases of non-conformity where national law still has to be brought into line with the requirements of the directive. An overview of the stage reached in proceedings in these cases is given in Annex IV, Part 3.

Among the most common subjects of complaint brought to the Commission's notice are: refusal by national authorities to provide the information requested, slowness of response, excessively broad interpretation by national government departments of the exceptions to the principle of disclosure, and unreasonably high charges. Directive 90/313/EEC is unusual in containing a requirement for Member States to put in place national remedies against the improper rejection or ignoring of requests for access to information or an unsatisfactory response by the authorities to such requests. When the Commission receives complaints about such cases, it normally advises the aggrieved parties to use the national channels of appeal established to allow the directive's aims to be achieved in practice.

2.8.3. Environmental impact assessment

(58) OJ L 197, 21.7.2001, p. 30.

Directive 85/337/EEC on the assessment of the effects of certain public and private projects on the environment, as amended by Directive 97/11/EC, is one of the prime legal instruments for general environmental matters. The directive requires environmental issues to be taken into account in many decisions which have a general impact. The deadline for transposition of Directive 97/11/EC amending Directive 85/337/EEC was 14 March 1999. Infringement cases concerning non-communication of the transposal measures are listed in Annex IV, Part 2.

Directive 2001/42/EC of the European Parliament and of the Council was adopted on 27 June 2001 ([58]). Member States must bring into force the national rules necessary to comply with this directive before 21 July 2004. Where Directive 85/337/EEC, which is a new 'strategic environmental assessment' directive of a procedural nature, applies to projects, the aim is to ensure that an environmental assessment is carried out for certain plans and programmes which are likely to have significant effects on the environment.

Problems with the conformity of national measures with the directive have persisted. An overview of the stage reached in infringement proceedings in these cases is given in Annex IV, Part 3.

In a judgment given on 14 June 2001 (Case C-230/00), the Court condemned Belgium for the possibility of granting tacit approvals for many types of plans and projects falling under the directive and certain other directives. The Court held that tacit authorisation cannot be compatible with Directive 85/337/EEC which requires assessment procedures preceding the grant of authorisation whereby the national authorities are required to examine individually every request for authorisation.

As already mentioned in previous reports on monitoring of the application of Community law, many complaints received by the Commission as well as oral and written questions tabled by the European Parliament and a large number of petitions presented to Parliament relate, at least incidentally, to alleged instances of incorrect application by Member States' authorities of Directive 85/337/EEC, in particular in cases concerning projects of the types listed in Annex II to the directive. These complaints often require the examination of whether Member States have exceeded their margin of discretion in deciding whether or not such projects should be subject to an environmental impact assessment. As regards complaints about the quality of impact assessments and the lack of weight given to them, it is extremely difficult for the Commission to assess these cases. The basically formal nature of the directive provides only a limited basis for contesting the merits of such assessments and the choice taken by the national authorities if they have complied with the procedure laid down by the directive. Most of the cases brought to the Commission's attention concerning incorrect application of this directive revolve around points of fact where the most effective evaluation should be ensured at a decentralised level, particularly through the competent national administrative and judicial bodies.

In the course of 2001 the Commission took action in a small number of cases involving incorrect application of the environmental assessment procedure in the context of individual infrastructure projects. An overview of the stage of proceedings reached in these infringement cases is given in Annex IV, Part 4.

2.8.4. Air

Council Directive 96/62/EC on ambient air-quality assessment and management forms the basis for a series of Community instruments to set new limit values for atmospheric pollutants, starting with those already covered by existing directives, lay down information and alert thresholds, harmonise air-quality assessment methods and improve air-quality management in order to protect human health and ecosystems.

Article 3 of the directive was due to be transposed by 21 May 1998. By the end of 2001, all Member States except Spain had complied with their obligation to notify measures implementing Article 3 of the directive. In a case brought by the Commission the Court condemned Spain for failing to adopt within the prescribed period the laws, regulations and administrative provisions necessary to designate the competent authorities and bodies referred to in the first paragraph of Article 3 of the directive (judgment of 13 September 2001 in Case C-417/99).

All the other articles of the directive had to be transposed by 19 July 2001. By the end of 2001 Belgium (Flanders), the United Kingdom, Ireland, Greece, Spain and Germany had still not notified the national implementing measures for those articles.

Five directives in the air sector were to be transposed by Member States during 2001. Infringement cases concerning non-communication of these directives are listed in Annex IV, Part 2.

Infringement action was taken due to problems of non-conformity in the air sector in a small number of cases (see Annex IV, Part 3).

2.8.5. Water

Monitoring implementation of Community legislation on water quality remains an important part of the Commission's work. This is due to the quantitative and qualitative importance of the responsibilities imposed on the Member States by Community law and by growing public concern about water quality.

There are several cases under way over infringements of Directive 75/440/EEC concerning the quality required of surface water intended for the abstraction of drinking water. Some of the proceedings concern the preparation of systematic action plans (Article 4(2)) as an essential part of the effort to safeguard water quality (nitrates, pesticides, etc.) Others are concerned with the criteria for exemptions under Article 4(3).

In its judgment of 8 March 2001 (Case C-266/99), the Court of Justice declared that, by failing to take the necessary measures to ensure that the quality of surface water intended for the abstraction of drinking water conforms to the values laid down pursuant to Article 3 of Directive 75/440/EEC, France had failed to fulfil its obligations under Article 4 of that directive. As France did not comply with the judgment, the Commission decided to send a letter of formal notice on the basis of Article 228 of the EC Treaty to France.

With regard to Directive 76/160/EEC concerning the quality of bathing water, monitoring of bathing areas is becoming increasingly common and water quality is improving. Despite this progress, however, proceedings are still under way against most Member States since implementation still falls far short of the directive's requirements. An overview of the stage reached in infringement proceedings in these cases is given in Annex IV, Part 4.

More information concerning the compliance with the parameters of water quality and sampling frequency of Directive 76/160/EEC is also provided by the annual reports on the quality of bathing water (see www.europa.eu.int/water/water-bathing/report).

In 2001, the Court condemned three Member States for insufficient water quality and/or sampling frequency: France (Case C-147/00, Judgment of 15 March 2001), the United Kingdom (Case C-427/00, Judgment of 13 November 2001) and Sweden (Case C-368/00, Judgment of 14 June 2001). The Commission continued court action against the Netherlands (Case C-268/00) and brought a similar action against Portugal (Case C-272/01) and Denmark (Case C-226/01).

Proceedings have been started against most Member States over their implementation of Directive 76/464/EEC on dangerous substances discharged into the aquatic environment and of the directives setting levels for individual substances.

The Court has given several judgments against Member States who have not yet notified sufficient measures to ensure compliance with Article 7 of the directive. An overview of the stage reached in proceedings in these and other infringement cases under Directive 76/464/EEC is given in Annex IV, Part 3 (non-conformity) and Part 4 (incorrect application).

The Commission intends to facilitate the adoption by the Member States of programmes under Article 7 of Directive 76/464/EEC by drafting a guidance document on this issue. With this document the Commission aims to support Member States in the implementation of both the existing directive and (Article 7 of Directive 76/464/EEC) and the new Water Framework Directive 2000/60/EC. The document will identify eight elements to be included in the programmes on pollution reduction.

Concerning Directive 80/778/EEC on drinking water, the Commission initiated and continued a small number of infringement cases relating to application of the directive, particularly concerning poor quality of drinking water. An overview of the stage of proceedings reached in these cases is given in Annex IV, Part 4.

Council Directive 98/83/EC of 3 November 1998 on the quality of water intended for human consumption, which will replace Directive 80/778/EEC from 2003 ([59]), was due to be transposed into national law by 25 December 2000. Member States may have to take steps immediately to ensure compliance with the new limit values under the new directive. Infringement cases concerning failure to notify implementing measures for this directive are listed in Annex IV, Part 2.

The Community has two legislative instruments aimed specifically at combating pollution from phosphates and nitrates and the eutrophication they cause.

The first, Directive 91/271/EEC, concerns urban wastewater treatment. Member States are required to ensure that, from 1998, 2000 or 2005, depending on population size, all cities have wastewater collection and treatment systems. In addition to checking notification and conformity of the implementing measures, the Commission must therefore now follow up cases of incorrect application. Since this directive plays a fundamental role in the campaign for clean water and against eutrophication, the Commission is particularly eager to ensure that it is implemented on time. During 2001, several infringement actions were taken due to insufficient designation of sensitive areas or non-compliance with the requirements for urban wastewater treatment. An overview of the stage of proceedings reached in these cases is given in Annex IV, Part 4.

The second anti–eutrophication measure is Directive 91/676/EEC concerning the protection of waters against pollution caused by nitrates from agricultural sources. The Commission has continued to lay great stress on enforcing

this directive. As it has done in the past, during 2001 the Commission took several infringement actions concerning lacking or insufficient designation of vulnerable zones as well as the failure to establish action programmes as required by the directive. Overview of the stage of proceedings in these cases is given in Annex IV, Part 4.

On 8 November 2001, the Court gave its judgment in the case against Italy over action programmes and reporting requirements (Case C-127/99). The Court condemned Italy for having failed to establish action programmes within the meaning of Article 5 of the directive, carry out the monitoring operations prescribed by Article 6, and to submit to the Commission a report under Article 10.

In its judgment of 8 March 2001, the Court condemned Luxembourg in Case C-266/00 for failing to adopt the implementing measures needed to comply with several provisions of the directive.

2.8.6. Nature

The two main legal instruments aimed at protecting nature are Directive 79/409/EEC on the conservation of wild birds and Directive 92/43/EEC on the conservation of natural habitats and of wild fauna and flora.

Regarding the transposal of Directive 79/409/EEC, several conformity problems remain unresolved. In 2001, the Commission had to continue infringement actions against many Member States, notably concerning hunting periods and hunting practices not in line with the directive.

In its judgment of 17 May 2001 (Case C-159/99) the Court found that, by laying down rules permitting the capture and keeping of the species *Passer italiae, Passer montanus* and *Sturnus vulgaris*, contrary to the combined provisions of Articles 5 and 7 of the directive, Italy had failed to fulfil its obligations under the directive.

The deadline for notifying the implementing measures for Directive 92/43/EEC expired in June 1994. In many cases the transposal is still insufficient, particularly concerning Article 6 on the protection of habitats in the special conservation sites which are to be set up, and Articles 12 to 16 on the protection of species.

As in the past, the main problems with the implementation of Directives 79/409/EEC and 92/43/EEC relate to the classification of special protection areas (SPA) for birds and the selection of the proposed sites of Community importance (SCI) for habitats for inclusion in the Natura 2000 network, or to the protection of such sites.

Existing SPAs for birds in a number of Member States are still too few in number or cover too small an area. The Commission's strategy revolves around initiating general infringement proceedings, rather than infringement pro-

([59]) OJ L 330, 5.12.1998, p. 32.

ceedings on a site-by-site basis. During 2001, the Commission continued infringement actions against France (Case C-202/01), Finland (Case C-240/00), Italy (Case C-378/01), Portugal, Spain and Luxembourg.

Member States continued to propose SCIs in accordance with Article 4(1) of Directive 92/43/EEC. During 2001, the Commission continued infringement proceedings against Austria, Belgium, Portugal, Sweden and the United Kingdom. The lists submitted by these Member States are either not satisfactory or are under assessment subject to the results of biogeographical seminars. In its judgment of 11 September 2001, the Court condemned Ireland (Case C-67/99), Germany (Case C-71/99) and France (Case C-220/99) for failing to transmit to the Commission, within the prescribed period, the list of sites mentioned in Article 4(1), first subparagraph, of Directive 92/43/EEC.

Problems remain concerning the special protection regime under Article 4(4) of Directive 79/409/EEC and Article 6(2) to (4) of Directive 92/43/EEC, e.g. wrongly applying or setting aside the special protection regime in relation to various projects affecting sites. In this respect, infringement actions against a number of Member States had to be taken in the course of 2001.

During 2001, the Commission continued setting conditions in Structural Fund plans and programmes and rural development programmes requiring Member States to submit outstanding lists for the setting up of the Natura 2000 network in accordance with their obligations under Directives 79/409/EEC and 92/43/EEC.

The Commission has maintained its strict policy with regard to the granting of Community funding for conservation of sites under the LIFE regulation on sites being integrated or already integrated into the Natura 2000 network. Furthermore, it scrutinises requests for co-financing from the Cohesion Fund very thoroughly for compliance with environmental regulations.

Problems with the implementation of Directive 92/43/EEC may also arise with regard to the protection, not of designated or nominated sites, but of species. Article 12 of the directive establishes a strict protection scheme for species under Annex IV (a), from which Member States can derogate only under the conditions laid down in Article 16(1) and (2). By the end of 2001, court actions were pending against Greece for threats to a species of turtle (*Caretta caretta*) on the island of Zakynthos (Case C-103/00) and against the United Kingdom for its failure to ensure the proper protection of the great crested newt (*Triturus cristatus*) (Case C-434/01). A reasoned opinion was sent to Germany for failure to properly protect the habitats of an endangered hamster (*Cricetus cricetus*) population at

Horbacher Börde near Aachen close to the border with the Netherlands, one of the most important sites for this species in north-west Germany.

2.8.7. Noise

Directive 2000/14/EC of the European Parliament and of the Council on the approximation of laws of the Member States relating to noise emission in the environment by equipment for use outdoors ([60]) was due to be transposed on 3 July 2001. This directive repeals, from 3 January 2002, nine directives concerning different types of equipment. The Commission had to start infringement proceedings against 13 Member States. By the end of 2001, infringement proceedings were still open against 11 Member States who had not yet adopted and notified their implementing measures, or had not done so for the whole of their territory.

2.8.8. Chemicals and biotechnology

Community legislation on chemicals and biotechnology covers various groups of directives relating to products or activities which have certain characteristics in common: they are technically complex, require frequent changes to adapt them to new knowledge, apply to both the scientific and industrial spheres and deal with specific environmental risks.

One of the features of Council Directive 67/548/EEC on the approximation of the laws, regulations and administrative provisions relating to the classification, packaging and labelling of dangerous substances is the frequency with which it has to be amended to keep up with scientific and technical developments. Thus, Commission Directive 2000/32/EC of 19 May 2000 adapting Directive 67/548/EEC to technical progress for the 26th time, had to be transposed by 1 June 2001. In addition, the transposal deadline for the Commission Directive 2000/21/EC of 25 April 2000 concerning the list of Community legislation referred to in the fifth indent of Article 13(1) of Directive 67/548/EEC was 1 April 2001.

In this context, Member States are still frequently late in notifying their implementing measures, but the Commission automatically commences proceedings in order to make Member States meet their obligations.

Directive 98/8/EC of the European Parliament and of the Council of 16 February 1998 concerning the placing on the market of biocidal products ([61]) was due to be transposed by the Member States by no later than 14 May 2000. At the end of 2001, there was still many Member States who had not yet notified their implementing measures, as demonstrated by the infringement cases listed under this directive in Annex IV, Part 2.

[60] *OJ L 162, 3.7.2000, p. 1.*

[61] *OJ L 123, 24.4.1998, p. 1.*

Animal experiments are covered by Directive 86/609/EEC on the approximation of laws, regulations and administrative provisions of the Member States regarding the protection of animals used for experimental and other scientific purposes. In its judgment of 18 October 2001, the Court found that Ireland had failed to adopt all the measures necessary to ensure the correct implementation of Articles 2(d), 11 and 12 of the directive as well as to provide for an adequate system of penalties for non-compliance with the requirements of the directive (Case C-354/99). A few infringement actions were continued against Member States as regards incorrect transposition and incorrect application of Directive 86/609/EEC (see Annex IV, Part 3 and Part 4 for the overview of the stage reached in these proceedings).

2.8.9. Waste

Infringement proceedings in relation to waste continue to abound, concerning both formal transposition and practical application. As mentioned in the last report, the most likely explanations for the difficulties in enforcing Community law in these matters are as much the need for changes in the conduct of private individuals, public services and business firms as the costs of such changes.

Regarding the framework directive on waste (Directive 75/442/EEC, as amended by Directive 91/156/EEC), the Member States still have problems in fully and correctly implementing its provisions into national law. An overview of the stage of proceedings reached in these cases is given in Annex IV, Part 3.

Most of the implementation difficulties concern the application of the waste framework directive to specific installations. This is at the root of the large number of complaints primarily concerned with waste dumping (uncontrolled dumps, controversial siting of planned controlled tips, mismanagement of lawful tips, water pollution caused by directly discharged waste). The directive requires that prior authorisation be obtained for waste-disposal and waste-reprocessing sites; in the case of waste disposal, the authorisation must lay down conditions to contain the environmental impact.

The adoption by the Council on 26 April 1999 of Directive 1999/31/EC on the landfill of waste (⁶²) clarifies the legal framework in which sites employing this method of disposal are authorised in the Member States. This directive was to be transposed by 16 July 2001. For landfills coming into operation after, as well as those existing on, this date, requirements have been tightened by this directive. The transposal of this directive by the Member States has been very slow, as demonstrated by the list of infringement

(⁶²) OJ L 182, 16.7.1999, p. 1.

cases concerning non-communication under this directive in Annex IV, Part 2.

As mentioned in previous reports, the Commission uses individual cases to detect more general problems concerning incorrect application of Community law, such as the absence or inadequacy of waste–management plans, based on the assumption that an illegal dump may provide evidence of an unsatisfied need for waste management.

In its judgment of 4 July 2000 (Case C-387/97), the Court decided to impose a financial penalty of EUR 20 000 per day on Greece for non-compliance with the judgment of the Court of 7 April 1992 (Case C-45/91). The case concerns the existence and the functioning of an illegal solid waste dump in Kouroupitos in the region of Chania where domestic waste, limited quantities of both dangerous waste (for example, waste oils and batteries) and different kinds of commercial and industrial waste were illegally dumped. The Commission has periodically sent the Greek authorities letters requesting payment of the daily penalty of EUR 20 000 from 4 July 2000 to February 2001 included. In March 2001, the site was closed and the waste was treated in an appropriate installation. Therefore, the Commission considered that Greece had complied with the judgment and closed the case. Greece has paid all the amounts due within the deadlines set, representing a total sum of EUR 5 400 000.

In addition, the Commission took a number of infringement actions involving incorrect application of the waste framework directive. These cases normally concern local problems relating to illegal landfills and/or uncontrolled treatment of waste, sometimes involving non-existent or insufficient environmental impact assessments.

Regarding Directive 91/689/EEC on hazardous waste, Member States still had problems in transposing the national legislation correctly.

Given that planning is such an important part of waste management, the Commission decided in October 1997 to start infringement proceedings against all Member States except Austria, the only State to have established a planning system for waste management. These proceedings are still continuing and cover a range of failings, relating variously to plans as required by Article 7 of the waste framework directive, plans for management of dangerous waste as required by Article 6 of Directive 91/689/EEC, and special plans for packaging waste, as required by Article 14 of Directive 94/62/EC.

In his opinion of 5 July 2001, the Advocate-General held that, by failing to draft waste management plans for the whole country for all categories of waste, and by failing to include a chapter on packaging waste in them, France has breached Article 7(1) of the waste framework directive, Article 6(1) of Directive 91/689/EEC and Article 14 of Directive 94/62/EC.

The Commission continued court actions brought earlier against the United Kingdom (Case C-35/00) and against Italy (Case C-466/99) in respect of all three categories of plans. In both cases the Advocate-General agreed with the Commission (opinion of Mr Mischo, 20 September 2001 in Case C-466/99 and opinion of Mr Tizzano, 11 September 2001 in Case C-35/00).

In its judgment of 11 December 2001, the Court stated that, by failing to forward to the Commission the report required for the period from 1995 to 1997 under Article 18 of Council Directive 75/439/EEC, as amended by Directive 91/692/EEC, within the period fixed by that provision, the Italian Republic had failed to fulfil its obligations under that directive (Case C-376/00).

As regards Directive 91/689/EEC on hazardous waste, the Commission had commenced infringement proceedings in 1998 against a number of Member States which had failed to provide the Commission with particular information required in relation to establishments or undertakings carrying out disposal and/or recovery of hazardous waste. In 2001, a court action against Greece (Case C-33/01) was brought on this point.

Regarding Directive 75/439/EEC on the disposal of waste oils, the Commission opened infringement proceedings against 11 Member States for the non-conformity of national legislation with several articles of the directive, particularly regarding the obligation to give priority to the processing of waste oils by regeneration, provided that technical, economic and organisational constraints so allowed. The Commission sent reasoned opinions to Austria, Ireland, Portugal and the United Kingdom, and the replies given by the France, Finland, Netherlands, Belgium, Sweden and Denmark to the letters of formal notice were being examined. The Commission also sent a letter of formal notice to Greece.

2.8.10. Environment and industry

Directive 96/82/EC (Seveso II), replacing Directive 82/501/EEC from 3 February 2001 (Seveso I), was due to be transposed by no later than 3 February 1999. The notification of implementing measures by many Member States is still incomplete, particularly as regards Articles 11 and 12 of the directive. Infringement cases concerning non-communication under this directive are listed in Annex IV, Part 2.

Directive 96/61/EC concerning integrated pollution prevention and control (IPPC), adopted on 24 September 1996, was due to be implemented by 30 October 1999. In the course of 2001, proceedings for non-communication of the transposition measures to the Commission still had to be continued, as demonstrated by the list of infringement cases under this directive in Annex IV, Part 2.

2.8.11. Radiation protection

In 2001, as well as in 2000, the number of submissions of national draft legislation under Article 33 of the Euratom Treaty was high because a large number of Member States were still working on the transposal of two main radiation protection directives, 96/29/Euratom and 97/43/Euratom, that should have been transposed by May 2000. The Commission received 13 submissions under Article 33 of the Euratom Treaty. Some of them have been examined and commented on, although no formal recommendation was issued during 2001. Nevertheless, in cases of late communication where an infringement procedure for non-communication was pending, the Member States were immediately informed that no recommendation would be issued, so that the national legislative procedure could be completed without delay.

Article 35 of the Euratom Treaty provides that each Member State must establish the facilities necessary to carry out continuous monitoring of the level of radioactivity in the air, water and soil and to ensure compliance with the basic standards. The Commission can verify the operation and efficiency of such facilities. During 2001, the Commission carried out one verification under Article 35 in Austria.

Article 37 aims to forestall radioactive contamination of the environment in another Member State, thereby protecting the general public against the dangers arising from ionising radiation. Accordingly, Member States must provide the Commission with general data relating to any plan for the disposal of radioactive waste. The Commission assesses the data in order to determine whether the implementation of the plan could cause radioactive contamination of the water, soil or airspace of another Member State. The Commission issues an opinion on the subject, which the Member State has to take into account prior to the authorisation for disposal of radioactive waste. The Commission received 17 submissions from Member States under Article 37 of the Euratom Treaty in 2001 and issued six opinions.

The Commission decided to send a reasoned opinion to the United Kingdom in December 2001 for failure to fulfil its obligations under Article 37, because it had not submitted the general data relating to dismantling of the JASON research reactor.

As mentioned above, the deadline for transposal of the two main directives in the area of radiation protection, Council

Directive 96/29/Euratom laying down basic safety standards for the health protection of the general public and workers against the dangers of ionising radiation (OJ L 159, 29.6.1996, p. 1) and Council Directive 97/43/Euratom on health protection of individuals against dangers of ionising radiation in relation to medical exposure (OJ L 180, 9.7.1997, p. 22), expired on 13 May 2000.

Directive 96/29/Euratom introduces a wider scope and a more detailed set of provisions in order to protect the health of workers and general public soundly and comprehensively. For this purpose, the directive reduced the dose limits, set new requirements for the justification of all practices involving ionising radiation and introduced an extended ALARA-principle, according to which doses must be kept 'As low as reasonably achievable'. The directive covers practices, work activities including natural radiation sources and intervention situations. It also clarifies the concept of clearance and exemption for materials containing radioactivity. Finally, the directive includes new requirements for the assessment of radiation doses for sections of the population. Infringement cases concerning failure to notify measures implementing this directive are listed in Annex IV, Part 2.

Directive 97/43/Euratom improves the level of radiological protection for patients and medical staff. It takes into account the new developments in medical procedures and equipment and the experience gained from the operational implementation of the former directives. It lays down a more precise description for the justification principle, regulates the distribution of responsibilities and sets requirements for qualified experts in the medical area. Infringement cases concerning failure to notify measures implementing this directive are listed in Annex IV, Part 2.

Directive 89/618/Euratom on informing the public includes requirements on informing the general public about health protection measures to be applied and steps to be taken in the event of radiological emergency. The Commission decided to refer France and Germany to the Court, since their legislation did not fully comply with the directive.

2.9. FISHERIES

Introduction

The Commission has continued to monitor the implementation by the Member States of the national legislative measures on resource conservation and management enacted under the common fisheries policy (measures to control fishing activities, technical conservation measures and technical measures applicable in the Mediterranean).

The Commission has not detected any cases of incompatibility of national measures with the Community legislation that could justify initiating infringement proceedings.

Resources

On 1 February 2001, the Court of Justice ruled against France [63], finding that it had failed to meet its obligations of control and inspection of fishing activities in 1988 and 1990.

Within the framework of proceedings for failure to comply with the control requirement by exceeding certain quotas allocated to Sweden and Ireland in 1995 and 1996, to Belgium in 1991, 1992, 1993, 1994, 1995 and 1996 and to Portugal in 1994, 1995 and 1996, the Commission sent reasoned opinions to these Member States on 20 February, 12 March, 31 July and 5 November respectively. The Commission also decided, on 18 July, to refer to the Court an appeal against Denmark based on overruns in 1990, 1991, 1992, 1993, 1994, 1995 and 1996.

2.10. INTERNAL MARKET

2.10.1. Free movement of goods

Application of Articles 28 et seq. EC
(ex-Articles 30 et seq. of the EC Treaty)

The volume of infringement dossiers on obstacles to trade (*application of Article 28 et seq.*) [64], remains relatively stable. However, litigation is becoming increasingly complex in technical terms because of the aspects relating to protection of public health, consumers or the environment. Several important cases in this area are pending before the Court of Justice, which should rule on them in 2002. The Commission's departments responsible for this litigation have continued to give priority to dialogue with the national authorities, notably in package meetings, so as not to have to use infringement proceedings except in cases where real disagreement persists. These package meetings have again proved their usefulness and effectiveness as a great many cases have been raised and dealt with. Practical seminars on the application of the principle of mutual recognition have also been organised in several of the countries that are candidates for accession. In view of their success and the fact that they have been recognised as being useful, other seminars will be organised in 2002 in the other candidate countries in order to improve the knowledge and practice of mutual recognition by their administrations.

[63] Case C-33/99, ECR 2001, p I-1025.

[64] See web page http://europa.eu.int/comm/internal_market/en/goods/mutrec.htm

The Commission also stepped up its activities providing information about and promoting *Decision 3052/95/EC* of the European Parliament and of the Council ([65]), pursuant to which the Member States are required to notify the Commission of national measures which constitute exceptions to the principle of the free movement of goods. The number of notifications received still appears to be insufficient. This finding, as well as certain proposals for improvements, had already been highlighted in the report on the implementation of the decision in 1997 and 1998 published by the Commission on 7 April 2000 ([66]).

As for the mechanism for *rapid intervention in the event of serious obstacles to the free movement of goods*, the warning system provided for in Article 3 of Council Regulation (EC) No 2679/98 of 7 December 1998 on the functioning of the internal market in relation to the free movement of goods ([67]) was used seven times in 2001, as compared with 18 in 2000.

Liability for defective products [Directive 85/374/EEC as amended ([68])]

All the Member States have transposed the amendment made by Directive 1999/34/EC ([69]), the purpose of which is to extend the rules of liability without fault to primary agricultural products. Also, on 31 January 2001 the Commission adopted the second report on the implementation of the directive ([70]).

2.10.2. Free movement of services and right of establishment

With regard to the **freedom to provide services** (Articles 43 and 49 et seq. of the EC Treaty) and within the framework of the implementation of its internal market strategy for services ([71]), the Commission has continued to process a considerable number of complaints made by undertakings or users of services in a wide variety of fields, such as security, accounting and audit services, bus transport, services provided by mountain guides, flying clubs, museums, health services provided by medical laboratories or pharmacies, aerial work, fairs, temping agencies, patent agents, artists, etc. Furthermore, as far as health services are concerned, the Court of Justice gave two judgments on 12 July 2001 (Cases C-157/99 and C-368/98) reinforcing the rights of insured persons regarding the reimbursement of the costs incurred for a surgical operation in another Member State. These rulings confirm the precedent established in Kohll et Decker ([72]) and make it clear that medical activities, including hospital services, do indeed fall within the scope of freedom to provide services. Furthermore, in the field of the information society and the media, on 29

November 2001 (Case C-17/00), responding to a request for a preliminary ruling, it issued a judgment declaring that taxes on parabolic antennas as imposed by certain communes in Belgium were not compatible with Article 49 of the EC Treaty, in line with the position adopted by the Commission in its communication of 27 June 2001 ([73]) and certain infringement proceedings on this subject ([74]).

In the field of **commercial communications,** the Commission is continuing its policy and has decided to refer to the Court of Justice the 'Loi Evin' case against France concerning restrictions on advertising and sponsorship services in the broadcasting of sports events by French television channels. By contrast, it has closed certain cases of infringements following the liberalisation of the German legislation on discounts and premiums.

As for the **media in the information society**, in 2001 the Commission sent seven reasoned opinions for failure to notify the national measures implementing Directive 98/84/EC of the European Council and of the Parliament on conditional access. In three cases, it decided to refer them to the Court.

As far as **financial services** are concerned, the *insurance* sector saw the relaunch of infringement proceedings on the no-claims bonus (France, Belgium, Finland and Luxembourg all received reasoned opinions on this subject in 2001) within the framework of the monitoring of the interpretative communication on the freedom to provide services and the general good. Two dossiers opened against Belgium and Finland on their legislation on insurance against accidents at work have been resolved. Finally, the process of transposing Directive 98/78/EC (insurance groups) is almost finished: only Greece, which is before the Court, and Portugal have still not notified their implementing measures.

In the field of *securities*, on 20 December 2001 the Commission referred an action to the Court against the United Kingdom for failure to fulfil its obligations of transposing, in the territory of Gibraltar, Directive 97/9/EC of the European Parliament and the Council on investor-compensation schemes ([75]).

As for *payment systems*, Regulation (EC) No 2560/2001 ([76]) on cross-border payments in euro was formally adopted on 19 December 2001 by the European Parliament and the Council on a proposal by the Commission of 25 July 2001 ([77]). This regulation aims to reduce bank charges for cross-border payments in euro, by aligning them on those which apply at national level. It comes into force on 1 January 2002. It is binding in its entirety and directly applicable in all Member States. The transposal of Directive 98/26/EC on settlement finality in payment and securities settlement systems should be complete by 11 December

([65]) OJ L 321, 30.12.1995, p. 1.

([66]) COM(2000) 194 final.

([67]) OJ L 337, 12.12.1998, p. 8.

([68]) OJ L 210, 7.08.1985, p. 29.

([69]) OJ L 141, 4.06.1999, p. 20.

([70]) COM(2000) 893 final (see also the site mentioned in footnote (64).

([71]) COM(2000) 888 final.

([72]) Case C-158/96, ECR 1998 p I-1931.

([73]) COM(2001) 351 final.

([74]) See IP 99/281 and 00/237.

([75]) OJ L 84, 26.3.1997, p. 22.

([76]) OJ L 344, 28.12.2001.

([77]) COM(2001) 439 final.

1999. All the Member States which had not notified their implementing measures in 1999 did so in 2001. The Commission has therefore been able to close the infringement proceedings.

2.10.3. The business environment

In the field of **intellectual property**, five Member States (Denmark, Finland, Greece, Ireland, the United Kingdom ([78])) notified their national implementing measures for Directive 98/44/EC on the legal protection of biological inventions. The Court of Justice issued an important ruling on 9 October 2001 (Case C-377/98) in which it rejected the action for annulment brought by the Netherlands against this directive.

As regards designs, the period for transposal of Directive 98/71/EC on the legal protection of designs expired on 28 October 2001. On 31 December 2001, three Member States (Denmark, France, Italy) notified the Commission of the national legal provisions which they adopted to comply with the directive.

In the field of copyright and related rights, there are six directives in force ([79]). All the Member States have notified their national measures implementing all the directives. Infringement proceedings have reached the reasoned opinion stage for Belgium, Denmark and the United Kingdom concerning Council Directive 92/100/EEC on rental right and lending right. Two own-initiative actions for infringements have been brought against Sweden and Finland regarding incorrect transposal of Directive 96/9/EC of the European Parliament and of the Council on the legal protection of databases. A case against Ireland was referred to the Court for its failure to ratify the Berne Convention (1971 Paris Act). The case (C-13/2000) is still pending and Ireland has still not notified its act of accession to the Convention.

The Commission continued to work towards a homogeneous, effective application of **public procurement** law in the Member States. To this end, it adopted two interpretative communications aiming to clarify the possibilities of incorporating environmental and social considerations into public procurement contracts ([80]). It also adopted a directive imposing the requirement to use standard forms in the publication of public contracts in the *Official Journal of the European Communities*, which will contribute to greater transparency and efficiency in public contracts and facilitate electronic contracts ([81]).

Generally speaking, the transposal of the 'public contracts' directives in the Member States has improved. However, the number of complaints for incorrect application has increased. In 2001, the Commission examined 356 complaints in the field of public contracts. A number of examples are given below.

In connection with a procedure to award a service contract for the installation of a radio communication system for the British police forces, the Commission took the view that, when the contracting authorities are drawing up technical specifications with reference to a European standard, they must also accept products and services which are equivalent in terms of their performance. Following discussions with the Commission, the British authorities eventually accepted the reasoning behind this position and adopted a circular in order to inform the contracting authorities accordingly.

Similarly, in an instruction to the contracting authorities, the British authorities took the view that the obligation to ensure genuine competition imposed by the Community directives for restricted invitations to tender was respected when the contracting body set the minimum number of tenderers at three. The Commission contested this interpretation and, on the basis of the *Commission* v *France* ruling ([82]), told the British authorities that the number of participants in a restricted invitation to tender could not be less than five. Consequently, following the Commission's intervention, the British authorities modified their instruction.

The European Commission also sent a reasoned opinion for failure to comply with a judgment declaring France to have failed to fulfil its obligation to completely transpose Directive 92/13/EEC (remedies in the utilities sectors). As a result, the French authorities finally notified their national measures implementing the directive.

In its 'Alcatel' judgment ([83]) on the Directive on Review Procedures (89/665/EEC), the Court ruled that the Member States were required to provide a review procedure enabling unsuccessful tenderers or candidates to have the decision awarding the contract set aside if it is unlawful, before the contract is signed, regardless of whether it is possible to obtain damages once the contract has been signed. Following this judgment, the Commission decided to refer Austria to the Court as four of its nine Länder — Salzburg, Styria, Lower Austria and Carinthia — have not yet adopted the measures needed to comply with the judgment.

The Commission launched infringement proceedings in connection with a public contract to build the new La Scala theatre in Milan, since it considered that the direct execution of infrastructure work offset against development charges due to the local authority gives rise to contracts for pecuniary interest which fall within the scope of the public procurement directives. Moreover, the Court of Justice also confirmed the Commission's position in its 'Scala' prelimi-

([78]) The United Kingdom has only partially transposed it (measures implementing Article 12 of the directive are still awaited).

([79]) 87/54/EEC (topographies of semi-conductor products), 91/250/EEC (computer programmes), 92/100/EEC (rental and lending rights), 93/83/EEC (cable and satellite), 93/98/EEC (term), 96/9/EC (databases).

([80]) Interpretative communication of the Commission on the Community law applicable to public procurement and the possibilities for integrating environmental considerations into public procurement and interpretative communication of the Commission on the Community law applicable to public procurement and the possibilities for integrating social considerations into public procurement, published in OJ No C 333, 28.11.2001.

([81]) Commission Directive 2001/78/EC of 13 September 2001 on the use of standard forms in the publication of public contract notices, OJ L 285, 29.10.2001.

([82]) Case C-225/98, judgment of 26 September 2000.

([83]) Commission Directive 2001/78/EC of 13 September 2001 on the use of standard forms in the publication of public contract notices, L 285, 29.10.2001.

nary ruling (⁸⁴). The Commission subsequently decided to send Italy a reasoned opinion.

Lastly, and in accordance with the Court of Justice's case law (⁸⁵), the Commission also examined the procedures for awarding public contracts and granting concessions for which the arrangements are not subject to the provisions of the public procurement directives, in order to establish whether they nonetheless respected the general rules and principles of the EC Treaty and in particular the principles of equal treatment and transparency. The Commission notes that, broadly speaking, this kind of examination is being carried out increasingly extensively.

For example, the Commission's departments were called on to examine whether the modalities of awarding a motorway concession to Portugal had been in conformity with the rules and principles of the EC Treaty and consistent with the interpretative communication (⁸⁶) on concessions under Community law published last year. No irregularity was found in this case.

As far as **company law and financial information is concerned**, the Commission opened infringement proceedings in an own-initiative case against the Dutch law 'Wet op de formeel buitenlandse vennootschappen' (WFBV). Articles 2, 3 and 4 of this law are incompatible with the EC Treaty – specifically, Articles 43 and 48 – in the sense that they impose discriminatory obligations on companies from other Member States which want to open branches in the Netherlands. Also, Articles 2 and 4(3) of the WFBV constitute infringements of Article 2 of the Eleventh Council Directive of 21 December 1989 concerning disclosure requirements in respect of branches opened in a Member State by certain types of company governed by the law of another State (⁸⁷), in that they specify additional obligations for companies from other Member States.

The Commission has registered a complaint against the German law *Aktiengesetz*. The complaint is that paragraphs 305 and 320b of this law are incompatible with the EC Treaty, notably its Article 43, on the grounds that these provisions disadvantage non-German public limited liability companies in certain transactions between public limited liability companies. The Commission is examining this complaint.

The Commission has also registered a complaint against the Spanish law on public limited liability companies (LSA). The complaint claims that Articles 158, 159 and 293 disadvantage shareholders of public limited liability companies in relation to the acquirers or holders of convertible bonds of these companies and also that they allegedly disadvantage minority shareholders of these companies in relation to majority shareholders.

2.10.4. Regulated professions (qualifications)

The volume of complaint and infringement files on the qualifications required for the regulated professions remains relatively stable. In 2001, about 20 complaints were referred to the Commission on restrictions contrary to both Articles 43 and 49 of the EC Treaty and the directives on the mutual recognition of professional qualifications. However, the litigation is becoming more complex. Also, in order to achieve more rapid solutions to some of the problems detected, the Commission has maintained regular contacts with the national authorities, in particular the experts in the groups and committees which have competence for this area.

2.11. REGIONAL POLICY

2.11.1. Analysis of causes

Regional policy is essentially governed by regulations which are directly applicable in the Member States. These regulations (cf. Regulation (EC) No 1260/99), in addition to those linked to financial control, lay down strict rules. Infringement cases concerning the rules on regional policy therefore relate either to incorrect application of the regulations or to irregularities (Article 1(2) of Council Regulation (EC, Euratom) No 2988/95 on financial management).

However, the irregularities also cover infringements of the provisions of other Community regulations. The existing link between measures relating to regional policy and compliance with all other Community legislation is also highlighted by the express obligation for activities receiving funding from the Structural Funds, the EIB or another existing financial instrument to comply with the provisions of the Treaty and acts adopted pursuant to it, as well as with Community policies (Article 8(1) of Regulation (EC) 1164/94 and Article 12 of Regulation (EEC) No 1260/99).

2.11.2. Effects of infringement situations

Proceedings are brought under Article 226 of the EC Treaty, in particular in cases of infringement of the provisions of the Structural Fund regulations (cf. collection of fees by the national bodies responsible for the management of aid arrangements co-financed by the Structural Funds, contrary to the provisions of these same regulations which require the total amount of funding to be paid to the final beneficiaries). As regards cases of 'irregularities', the Commission can open specific proceedings with a view to suspending, reducing or cancelling the financial assistance from the Fund

(⁸⁴) *Case C-399/98, judgment of 12 July 2001.*

(⁸⁵) *See Case C-324/98, Telaustria, judgment of 7 December 2000 (regarding public service concessions), Case C-59/00, Vestergaard, order of 3 December 2001 (regarding public contracts with a value below the threshold values specified).*

(⁸⁶) *Communication published in OJ C 121, 29.4.2000, p. 2.*

(⁸⁷) *89/666/EEC, OJ No L 395, 30.12.1989, p. 36.*

concerned in accordance with Article 24 of Regulation (EEC) No 4253/88 (as amended by Regulation (EEC) No 2082/93), as well as Article 38(5) and Article 39 of Regulation (EC) No 1260/99. Such proceedings were initiated, for example, against Greece in the case of the granting of Community financial assistance under the ERDF OP, which is part of the Community support framework for Community structural interventions in the zones eligible for Objective 1.

2.12. TAXATION AND CUSTOMS UNION

2.12.1. Customs union

In the customs field, Community legislation mainly takes the form of regulations, so the question of how it is incorporated into national law does not arise and, in general terms, it can be said that the provisions in this area have been well integrated at national level.

Infringement proceedings are therefore fairly isolated. Two were launched in 2001.

– France: The Commission was compelled to initiate infringement proceedings against France regarding legislation requiring pilots of small aircraft on intra-Community flights to land first at an airfield with a customs office or to give 24 or 48 hours notice before take-off. Regulation (EEC) No 3925/91 [88] forbids checks and formalities on the baggage of travellers taking intra-Community flights, while allowing exceptional checks. Moreover, in France the pilot is sometimes charged for the travel expenses of the service carrying out the checks, and that constitutes a charge equivalent to a customs duty, which is illegal under Articles 23 and 25 of the EC Treaty.

– Greece: Greece introduced a new tax on private pleasure craft entering Greek territorial waters which are more than 7m in length and which have no permanent mooring in a Greek port. The tax is levied each time a pleasure boat enters the country and approaches a Greek port, harbour or coast; the amount is calculated on the length of the boat and comes on top of any harbour dues normally levied. It is paid into the special account of the Harbour Police Fund. As this tax does not relate to a service actually rendered to the person paying it is a tax with equivalent effect to import duties contrary to Articles 23 and 25 of the EC Treaty. It is prohibited irrespective of whether it is levied on Community pleasure craft or third country pleasure craft (pursuant to Articles 23, 25 and 133 of the EC Treaty).

2.12.2. Direct taxation

The almost total lack of harmonisation in this sector means that questions continually arise over the compliance of national provisions with primary Community legislation, whether as a result of complaints to the Commission, the European Parliament or the national courts, which are sending more and more cases to the Court for a preliminary ruling. To help find consensual solutions to infringement proceedings, the Commission has suggested to the Member States that they should discuss common problems with each other [89]. Systematic intervention by the Commission in cases referred for a preliminary ruling is therefore the most important control mechanism in this area.

Tax obstacles to the freedom to provide services in the supplementary insurance sector prompted the Commission to adopt a communication to help persons concerned to take advantage of their rights, which are protected under the Treaty [90] (a case has been referred by the Swedish courts for a preliminary ruling [91]). To ensure that citizens and investment companies reap the benefits of the internal market, and in line with its action plan on financial services, the Commission also reminded the Member States of the consequences of the Verkooijen case of 6 June 2000 [92] for restrictions on foreign investment. It initiated infringement proceedings against France and Belgium for failure to respect the freedom of capital movements (tax advantages for pensions savings conditional on investment in national securities) and welcomes the fact that these matters are currently being rectified by legislative amendments in the Member States concerned, without the necessity for the Court of Justice to become involved. Similarly, following action taken by the Commission, Spain adopted new legislation to end its refusal to accept the depreciation of capital gains in the case of securities purchased by non-residents, in violation of Articles 43 and 56 of the Treaty.

The judgment of 8 March 2001 in the *Metallgesellschaft* and *Hoechst* [93] joined cases illustrates the boundaries Member States should respect under the terms of the Treaty (freedom of establishment), if they wish to treat subsidiaries of national companies differently from those of other Member States as regards tax. However, the Court did not rule on the question also raised by these cases of whether the EC Treaty should be interpreted in such a way as to conclude that the advantages contained in bilateral tax conventions should be extended to all the other Member States.

Complainants most often cite the differences in the tax system applied to residents and non-residents, which they consider to be discriminatory. However, while the Court of

[88] OJ L 374, 31.12.1991, p. 4.

[89] See Communication from the Commission to the Council, the European Parliament and the Economic and Social Committee: tax policy in the European Union — priorities for the years ahead (presented on 23.5.2001 — COM(2001) 260 final, OJ C 284, 10.10.2001, p. 6.

[90] COM(2001)214, OJ C 165, 8.6.2001, p. 14.

[91] Case C-422/2001, Ramstedt and Skandia.

[92] Case C-35/1998.

[93] Cases C-397/1998 and 410/1998.

Justice has accepted in principle that the situation of residents and non-residents is usually different and that therefore different tax systems may be justified [94], the distinctions must be based on relevant factors.

The Commission took court action against Germany regarding a flat-rate and final tax on foreign artists, who were not allowed to deduct professional expenditure [95].

Tax treatment of inheritance for foreign nationals, which is different from that applied to nationals, is the subject of complaints against many Member States. In a new case before the Court, referred by a Dutch court [96], the Commission emphasised that the free movement of persons must also be respected in this area.

2.12.3. Value added tax

The Commission has had to initiate several new proceedings concerning failure to apply correctly the provisions of the Sixth VAT Directive (77/388/EEC) [97] with regard to the uniform basis of assessment.

– Germany, Belgium, Luxembourg, the Netherlands: under Article 2 of the Sixth Directive, deliveries of goods by a taxable person are taxable in the country concerned. The four Member States concerned, however, exempt from VAT supplies to barges engaged in international transport, even though there is no specific provision for such an exemption in the Sixth Directive.

– France: the Commission considers that French legislation allowing a pro rata deduction to taxable persons engaged solely in taxed operations, while maintaining a special rule limiting deductibility of VAT in respect of the purchase of goods or services because they were financed through grants, contravenes Articles 17(2), 17(5) and 19 of the directive.

– Greece: Greek legislation does not comply with Article 13(1) of the directive in that it excludes from the exemption the provision of services directly relating to teaching activities, such as school transport, carried out by bodies governed by public law or recognised by the State as having a comparable status.

The Commission also made referrals to the Court in several proceedings already initiated.

– Finland, Italy: non-taxation of Community aid for dried fodder, even though it should be considered as being directly linked to the price and, consequently, included in the taxable VAT base [98].

– France: application of two VAT rates (one on the subscription and another on the kilowatts of power consumed) to gas and electricity [99].

– Spain: application of a reduced rate of VAT on supplies of bottled gas and deliveries of mopeds [100].

Finally, a significant number of proceedings were closed after the Member States concerned modified their legislation as a result of the Commission's action.

– France: as requested by the Court in its judgment of 29 March 2001 [101], France now includes compulsory service charges in the VAT assessment base. Moreover, pursuant to the Court's judgment of 11 January 2001 [102], the fees charged for sending the results of medical analyses between laboratories are now exempt from VAT.

– Ireland, France: national measures have been taken by the two Member States concerned to make tolls on motorways subject to VAT, in line with the Court's ruling of 12 September 2000 [103].

– Spain: Spain now includes in the VAT assessment base Community aid to processing firms manufacturing dried animal feed.

– Netherlands: the Netherlands now applies a single tax rate to water supplies, as the Sixth Directive stipulates that an individual product may not attract several different rates of tax.

Finally, the proceedings initiated against France for violation of the provisions of the Eighth VAT Directive (79/1072/EC) [104] regarding the arrangements for the refund of VAT to taxable persons not registered in the territory of the country, were closed after national legislation in the field was amended. The Court found against France on 25 January 2001 because of its refusal to refund VAT to taxable persons not established in France, in cases where those taxable persons had subcontracted part of their work, relating to the disposal of waste, to a taxable person established in France [105].

2.12.4. Other indirect taxes

There are now quite a number of Community provisions on indirect taxation, concerning all categories of European citizens, who can take direct advantage of these provisions before national courts when confronted by cases of infringement of Community law in a Member State. Moreover, the Commission noted a fourfold increase in the number of complaints in this area in 2001, many of them concerning the United Kingdom, which applies to travellers returning from other Member States where they have bought alcohol or tobacco for their own personal use, sanctions which may be incompatible with the provisions of Directive 92/12/EC [106] on the general arrangements for products subject to excise duty.

[94] Judgment of 14.2.1995 in Case C-279/93, Schumacker.

[95] Case C-234/01, Gerritse.

[96] Case C-364/01, Barbier.

[97] OJ L 145, 13.6.1977, p. 1.

[98] Cases C-381/2001 and C-495/2001.

[99] Case C-384/2001.

[100] Cases C-143/2001 and C-144/2001.

[101] Case C-404/1999.

[102] Case C-76/1999.

[103] Cases C-276/1997 and C-358/1997.

[104] OJ L 331, 27.12.1979, p. 11.

[105] Case 429/1997.

[106] OJ L 76, 23.3.1992, p. 1.

Also in the sector of excise duty on alcohol and tobacco, the following points should be mentioned.

– Initiation of proceedings against Sweden, which applies different rates of tax, in violation of Article 90(2) of the Treaty, to wine and beer, since the current system protects a nationally produced product (beer) rather than similar products from other Member States (wine).

– Referral to the Court of the Greek arrangements for preferential taxation of ouzo ([107]).

– Closure of the proceedings initiated against Greece and Belgium concerning excise duty on tobacco products, following amendments to the legislation to bring it into line with the directives concerned.

In the sector of harmonised excise duty on mineral oils, one case was referred to the Court concerning incorrect application by Germany of Directive 92/81/EC ([108]) as regards taxation of heating oil ([109]), and another concerning incorrect application by Italy of Directive 92/82/EC ([110]), which applied a tax on lubricants when such products should be exempt from duty ([111]).

The number of complaints registered in the vehicle tax sector also soared in the reference year, this being a very sensitive area in the eyes of European citizens, particularly where problems relating to a change of residence are concerned. The Commission is aware of these difficulties and will soon present a report on vehicle taxation in the Community, while continuing to ensure that the Treaty provisions are strictly observed and that case law in the field is reinforced. In this connection, the Commission also reminded all the Member States of the consequences of the *Gomes Valente* judgment of 22 February 2001 on the taxation of second-hand cars ([112]). The proceedings initiated against France for applying discriminatory taxation, within the meaning of Article 90 of the EC Treaty, to cars equipped with 5-gear automatic gearboxes or 6-gear manual gearboxes, were closed after France took steps to comply with the Court's judgment of 15 March 2001 ([113]).

2.13. EDUCATION, AUDIOVISUAL MEDIA AND CULTURE

2.13.1. Education

In the field of education, Article 12 of the EC Treaty stipulates that the Member States must refrain from direct or indirect discrimination on the grounds of nationality, as regards access to education. Infringement proceedings

dealt with by the Directorate-General for Education and Culture in 2001 were in the following areas:

– higher enrolment fees in public educational establishments for nationals of other Member States than for nationals of the host country;

– different conditions of access to education for holders of diplomas from other Member States and holders of national diplomas (e.g.: aptitude tests, etc.);

– numerus clausus systems for access to higher education imposed on holders of foreign diplomas only, or in such a way as to discriminate against holders of foreign diplomas by comparison with holders of national diplomas;

– failure to take into account professional experience acquired in other Member States or diplomas conferred in other Member States as a result of professional examinations giving access to a particular profession or at the time of access to education.

Reasoned opinions were addressed to Belgium and Austria regarding the imposition of different access criteria for holders of national diplomas and holders of diplomas from other Member States. In their reply, the Belgian authorities agreed to amend the relevant national legislation.

Some of the reasons why Member States fail to comply with Article 12, as interpreted by Court of Justice case law, are as follows.

– Member States which do not operate a numerus clausus system for national students are faced with financial difficulties when they have to accept students from other Member States on the same terms as their own. For this reason, they try to apply stricter selection systems to nationals of other Member States. National systems of financing higher education are often at the root of the financial difficulties encountered by public institutions.

– The field of academic recognition of diplomas is also one which is often misinterpreted. According to the Treaty, the Member States are responsible for the educational content and organisation of their education systems. Some Member States consider that the recognition of diplomas is inextricably linked to that autonomy. Policies or administrative practices which protect national diplomas and do not respect the principle of non-discrimination are therefore applied. In these cases, the Commission insists that the relevant national legislation be amended to conform with the fundamental principle of Article 12 of the Treaty.

The Directorate-General for Education and Culture receives many letters from citizens relating to the recognition of diplomas, an area in which – as explained above –

([107]) Case C-475/2001.

([108]) OJ L 316, 31.10.1992, p. 12.

([109]) Case C–240/2001.

([110]) OJ 316, 31.10.92, p. 19.

([111]) Case C-437/2001.

([112]) Case C-393/1998.

([113]) Case C-265/1999.

Community competence is limited. The Commission informs the parties concerned in these cases of their rights under Community law and suggests, for cases which are not within the Community's remit, the use of national appeal systems. Other obstacles to student mobility reported to the Commission include administrative hurdles such as slowness, cost of procedures, etc.

2.13.2. Audiovisual media

Directives 97/36/EC of 30 June 1997 and 89/552/EEC of 3 October 1989 (Television without frontiers)

2.13.2.1. Progress in transposing the revised directive

The Commission's first priority as guardian of the Treaties is to ensure that directive 97/36/EC of 30 June 1997, amending the 1989 directive, is properly transposed. The date for transposal of the directive was 30 December 1998. At the time of writing 14 Member States had correctly notified national measures implementing Directive 97/36/EC. In 2001 the Court of Justice in two cases decided that the Member State had not implemented the directive in time. The Court stated that Luxembourg ([114]) and Italy ([115]) had failed to fulfil their obligations under the directive. In both Member States the provisions of the directive have been duly implemented in the meantime. A case against the Netherlands ([116]) was withdrawn as the Netherlands has now transposed the directive in substance.

2.13.2.2. Application of the directive

The revised directive establishes a solid legal framework for television broadcasters to develop their activities in the European Union. The main objective is to create the conditions for the free movement of television programmes. The revised directive clarifies a number of provisions, including the principle of regulation by the broadcaster's country of origin and the criteria for connecting broadcasters to a particular country's jurisdiction. The Commission enforced these principles during the report period. The Commission has been informed of a new decision by the Dutch authorities (*Commissariaat voor de Media*) to require RTL 4 and RTL 5 to apply for a Dutch licence. This decision confirms their previous decision of 20 November 1997. The contact committee on the 'Television without frontiers' directive discussed the case in its meeting of 20 September 2001 following the first decision of the *Commissariaat voor de Media* and the successive court proceedings in the Netherlands. The Commission argued at that meeting that the Dutch position was incompatible with Community law. Article 3a(1) of the directive provides the Member States with a legal basis for taking national measures to protect a number of events regarded as being of major importance to society. Measures based on Article 3a(1) were taken by Denmark (OJ C 14, 19.1.1999), Italy (OJ C 277, 30.9.1999), Germany (OJ C 277, 29.9.2000), the United Kingdom (OJ C 328, 18.11.2000) and Austria (OJ C 16, 19.1.2002). Belgium, the Netherlands and France have stated that they are planning to notify the Commission of draft measures in the near future. Denmark revoked its list at the end of the report period. Article 3a has been the subject of a judgment by the House of Lords ([117]), which found that 'the result which Article 3a(3) requires Member States to achieve is perfectly clear. It is to prevent the exercise by broadcasters of exclusive rights in such a way that a substantial proportion of the public in another Member State is deprived of the possibility of following a designated event.' Another case is pending before the European Court of First Instance ([118]).

The directive also lays down rules on the quantity of advertising authorised. The Commission received several complaints about alleged failures to comply with the advertising and sponsorship rules in the Member States. Problems arose in particular with the practices of certain broadcasters in Greece, Spain, Italy and Portugal. The Commission is analysing the situation in these countries to find out whether the alleged excesses might constitute infringements by the relevant Member. As a result the Commission decided to send a reasoned opinion to Spain (21 December 2000). In the preliminary ruling procedure C-245/01, *RTL Television*, the Commission delivered a written observation on 12 November on the interpretation of Article 11(3) of the directive.

By way of exception from the general rule of freedom to receive and retransmit, Article 2a(2) of the directive allows the Member States, subject to a specific procedure, to take measures against broadcasters under the jurisdiction of another Member State who 'manifestly, seriously and gravely' infringe Article 22. The aim is to protect minors against programmes 'likely to impair (their) physical, mental or moral development' and to 'ensure that broadcasts do not contain any incitement to hatred on grounds of race, sex, religion or nationality'. The Commission considers that Article 2a(2) was satisfactorily applied during the report period.

2.13.2.3. Enlargement-related questions

Since 2000, applicant countries have made further progress in aligning their legislation on the directive. Nine applicant countries have now reached a high level of alignment with the Community *acquis* (Bulgaria, Cyprus, Czech Republic, Estonia, Latvia, Lithuania, Malta, Slovak Republic and Slovenia). Good progress has also been made in Poland, where a complementary legislative process is

([114]) *Judgement of the Court (Fourth Chamber) of 21 June 2001. Commission of the European Communities v Grand Duchy of Luxembourg. Failure by a Member State to fulfil its obligations — Failure to implement Directive 97/36/EC amending Directive 89/552/EEC — Coordination of certain provisions laid down by law, regulation or administrative action in Member States concerning the pursuit of television broadcasting activities. Case C-119/00.*

([115]) *Judgement of the Court (Fourth Chamber) of 14 June 2001. Commission of the European Communities v Italian Republic. Failure by a Member State to fulfil its obligations — Failure to implement Directive 97/36/EC amending Directive 89/552/EEC — Coordination of certain provisions laid down by law, regulation or administrative action in Member States concerning the pursuit of television broadcasting activities. Case C-207/00.*

([116]) *Case C-145/00.*

([117]) *Regina v ITC, 25 July 2001, UKHL 42.*

([118]) *Case T-33/01, Kirch Media and KirchMedia WM v Commission. The application requests the annulment of the 'decision' of the Commission of 18 November 2000 under Article 3a of the directive. The Commission found compatible with Community law UK measures prohibiting broadcasters from broadcasting certain listed sporting events in a way that deprived a substantial proportion of the United Kingdom from viewing them and communicated the UK measures to the other Member States in order to ensure that broadcasters within their respective jurisdictions comply with the UK measures.*

under way. New legislation still has to be enacted in Hungary, Romania and Turkey.

2.14. HEALTH AND CONSUMER PROTECTION

2.14.1. Veterinary legislation

Regarding the *notification of national implementing measures*, only Directive 2001/10/EC as regards scrapie fell due for transposal in 2001. Greece, France, Italy, Portugal and Sweden still have to transpose this directive.

Most Member States have no further procedures for non-communication outstanding in this sector. Greece and France have made an effort to reduce delays in transposal; however, procedures initiated in previous years still have to be completed.

In matters other than the failure to notify of transposal measures, the most important event was the judgment adopted on 13 December 2001 in Case C-1/00 in which the Court concluded that France had failed to fulfil its obligations under Decisions 98/256/EC and 1999/514/EC by its refusal to permit the marketing on its territory of products subject to the date based export scheme which were correctly marked or labelled. The DBES had been set up to ensure that beef products exported from the United Kingdom had not been infected with BSE. The DBES scheme and the possibility of applying traceability arrangements on its territory were considered by the Court to be sufficient to provide France with the guarantees it needed to allow the import of British beef which met the requirements of the DBES.

In the light of this judgment, France must now regularise the infringement.

In another highly sensitive matter, namely the infringement proceedings initiated in 1999 against Belgium for failure to fulfil its obligations under Directives 89/662/EEC and 90/425/EEC to notify the Commission immediately of any circumstances likely to constitute a serious hazard to animals or humans, the Commission, having received confirmation from the Belgian Government that it shared the Commission's interpretation of the provisions concerned and an undertaking that there would be no recurrence of such an infringement, decided that the infringement proceedings had had the desired effect. It consequently closed the proceedings in question.

Two infringement proceedings initiated against the United Kingdom seem to be moving towards a satisfactory conclusion. On the question of inadequate veterinary supervision of abattoirs due to a shortage of veterinary officers,

the Commission established that the British authorities had made an effort to ensure that Community requirements in this matter were properly applied. The Commission is currently verifying whether the United Kingdom is now, as it claims, in a position to provide adequate veterinary inspections in all abattoirs, cutting plants and cold stores.

The Commission has been informed that the United Kingdom has put an end to the infringement whereby abattoirs were authorised to use hyperchlorinated water to disinfect poultry carcasses. As soon as the Commission has proof that this infringement has been corrected this case can also be closed.

In the case of France, the Commission has sent a supplementary letter of formal notice extending the infringement proceedings initiated for dispensation from health approval for certain establishments selling meat or meat products.

Based on an inspection report by the Food and Veterinary Office, the Commission decided to refer to the Court the fact that France had not withdrawn health approval from an abattoir which did not meet the requirements of Directive 64/433/EEC.

Still in the veterinary sector, the Commission continued, with a reasoned opinion, the infringement proceedings it had initiated against Sweden for continuing to obstruct intra-Community trade in meat and meat products by requiring prior notification of arrivals of the products concerned from the other Member States.

2.14.2. Plant health legislation

Regarding Member States' notification of national implementing measures, Denmark, Spain and Ireland notified measures transposing all the directives in this area which were due for transposal in 2001.

On the other hand, there are many transposal delays in Germany, Austria and France.

In the United Kingdom the devolution of legislative powers is a particular cause of transposal delays in this area.

The only infringement case for failure to transpose legislation properly has been closed, Italy having complied with the Commission's reasoned opinion.

2.14.3. Legislation on seeds and plants

No directives fell due for transposal in 2001. The infringement procedures relate to earlier years.

The Commission took Germany to court for failure to transpose Directive 98/56/EC on the marketing of propagating material of ornamental plants (Case C-2001/135); the German authorities must enact a law and implementing measures in order to reduce the delays in transposal of the other directives in this sector.

The Commission also took Greece to court for failure to transpose Directive 1999/8/EC on the marketing of cereal seed (Case C-2001/450).

2.14.4. Food legislation

Relatively few problems remain in this area as regards notification by Member States of national implementing measures.

2.14.5. Animal feedingstuffs legislation

Regarding the *notification of national measures implementing directives*, the only directive falling due for transposal in 2001 was Directive 2000/16/EC of the European Parliament and the Council of 10 April 2000 amending Council Directive 79/373/EEC on the marketing of compound feedingstuffs and Council Directive 96/25/EC on the circulation of feed materials. Most Member States have not yet notified their transposal measures.

Greece has the largest transposal backlog. The Court ruled against Greece for failing to fulfil its obligation to transpose five directives on animal feedstuffs. Greece complied with two Court rulings, enabling the Commission to close the Article 228 infringement case concerning the failure to adopt Directive 96/25/EC on the circulation of feed materials. The three judgments on Directives 95/69/EC and 98/51/EC on the registration of certain establishments in the animal feed sector, and Directive 96/24/EC on the marketing of compound feedingstuffs still have to be implemented, however.

Italy complied with two Court judgments that it had failed to fulfil its obligation to transpose Directives 96/51/EC and 98/51/EC; the Commission was able to close these cases.

2.14.6. Consumer protection

In this sector, the Commission's departments noted an improvement in transposal rates. France, Luxembourg and the Netherlands have not transposed all the directives which fell due. Cases have been brought before the Court for non-transposal by Spain of Directives 97/7/EC (distance contracts), 97/55/EC (misleading advertising) and 98/7/EC (consumer credit).

In the following four judgments the Court clarified Community legislation in the field of consumers' legal and economic interests.

In Case C-144/99 *Commission v the Netherlands*, the Court, in on the action brought by the Commission, found that the Netherlands, by failing to adopt the provisions necessary for the full transposition into Dutch law of Articles 4(2) and 5 of Council Directive 93/13/EEC on unfair terms in consumer contracts, had failed to fulfil its obligations under the said directive: whilst legislative action on the part of each Member State was not necessarily required in order to implement a directive, it was essential for national law to guarantee that the national authorities would effectively apply the directive in full, that the legal position under national law should be sufficiently precise and clear and that individuals were made fully aware of their rights and, where appropriate, might rely on them before the national courts.

In Case C-481/99 *Heininger v Bayerische Hypo- und Vereinsbank AG*, it was ruled that Council Directive 85/577/EEC to protect the consumer in respect of contracts negotiated away from business premises should be interpreted as applying to a secured-credit agreement, with the result that a consumer who has entered into an agreement of that type in one of the cases specified in Article 1 has the right to cancel that agreement, as provided for in Article 5. According to this decision, a loan taken out to finance the purchase of a flat and secured by means of a *Grundschuld* (charge on the property) in the same amount did not constitute a 'contract for the construction, sale and rental of immovable property or contract concerning other rights relating to immovable property' and hence was excluded from the scope of the directive.

The Court's judgment in Case C-112/99 *Toshiba Europe GmbH v Katun Germany GmbH* contains initial clarification on Community legislation on comparative advertising: the indication, in the catalogue of a supplier of spare parts and consumable items suitable for the products of an equipment manufacturer, of product numbers (OEM numbers) by which the equipment manufacturer designates the spare parts and consumable items which he himself sells may constitute comparative advertising which objectively compares one or more material, relevant, verifiable and representative features of goods. Article 3a(1)(g) of Directive 84/450 as amended by Directive 97/55/EC, should be interpreted to mean that where product numbers (OEM numbers) of an equipment manufacturer are, as such, distinguishing marks within the meaning of that provision, their use in the catalogues of a competing supplier enables him to take unfair advantage of the reputation attached to those marks only if the effect of the reference to them is to create, in the mind of the persons at whom the advertising is directed, an association between the manufacturer whose products are identified and the competing supplier, in that those persons associate the reputation of the manufacturer's products with the products of the competing supplier. In order to determine whether that condition is satisfied, account should be taken of the overall presentation of the advertising at issue and the type of persons for whom the advertising is intended.

In joined Cases C-541/99 and C-542/99 *Cape Snc v Idealservice Srl* and *Idealservice MN RE Sas* v *OMAI Srl*, it was made clear that the term 'consumer' as defined in Article 2(b) of Directive 93/13/EEC on unfair terms in consumer contracts must be interpreted as referring solely to natural persons.

2.14.7. Notification of technical rules

Directive 98/34/EC requires the Member States and the EFTA countries to notify each other and the Commission prior to the adoption of all drafts of instruments laying down technical standards or rules so as to avoid new barriers being raised in the internal market. Health (including food) was the area in which the Commission received the largest number of notifications in 2001.

(For more details see Chapter 2.2.6 on the application of Directive 98/34/EC).

2.15. JUSTICE AND HOME AFFAIRS

2.15.1. Establishment of an area of freedom, security and justice

The Treaty of Amsterdam incorporated in the Treaties the new objective of establishing the Union as an area of freedom, security and justice. Since 1 May 1999, and in accordance with the conclusions of the Tampere European Council, work has begun on legislation to create the instruments required for the implementation of this objective (¹¹⁹). A number of instruments have already been approved on the basis of Title IV of the EC Treaty, which covers those areas brought within the Community's area of competence by the Treaty of Amsterdam, such as visas, internal and external borders, asylum and immigration, and judicial cooperation in civil matters. The application of these instruments is monitored within the Community institutional framework. Some of these instruments replaced acts adopted before the entry into force of the Amsterdam Treaty under Title VI of the Treaty on European Union or within an intergovernmental framework and which consequently eluded the Community mechanisms for monitoring application.

The Commission had already pointed out in its eighteenth report on the monitoring of the application of Community law (¹²⁰) that provisions of the Schengen *acquis* allocated to the first pillar (¹²¹) were monitored in accordance with

the principles of Community law and that failure to respect these provisions could lead to infringement proceedings.

2.15.2. Monitoring the application of instruments based on Title VI of the EU Treaty

Measures in the field of police and judicial cooperation in criminal matters required for the establishment of an area of freedom, security and justice are adopted under Title VI of the EU Treaty. Articles 226 and 227 of the EC Treaty do not apply to the third pillar, so in the past the Council retained responsibility for monitoring transposal into national law and the application of the instruments in question. However, most recent instruments based on Title VI of the EU Treaty included the provision that the Commission should also ensure the proper transposal and application of the measure in question and table a report (¹²²). This represents a definite improvement, as the report can be used to impose political penalties for failure to comply with the instrument concerned.

2.15.3. The Charter of Fundamental Rights

The Charter of Fundamental Rights of the European Union (¹²³) reaffirms, with due regard for the powers and tasks of the Community and the Union the rights as they result, in particular, from the constitutional traditions and international obligations common to the Member States. The status of the Charter and the question of its integration in the Treaties will be examined by the convention on the future of Europe.

The charter is not at the moment a legally binding instrument and cannot therefore be used as the basis for an infringement procedure.

It should be pointed out, however, that the mechanisms for penalising failure to comply with Community law, such as the infringement procedure, can be initiated in respect of an infringement of a fundamental right under the EC Treaty as a general principle of Community law.

2.15.4. The right of citizens of the Union to move freely

The right of citizens of the Union (and members of their family) to move freely within the territory of the Member States derives directly from the EC Treaty and is governed by 12 instruments of secondary legislation applicable to different categories of citizens of the Union. A large number of complaints have been received concerning the application of this secondary legislation. In order to ensure that all Union citizens enjoy the same rights of entry and residence whatever their status (student, worker in gainful employment, pensioner, etc.), to make it easier to exercise the right to

(¹¹⁹) See the Commission's scoreboard to review progress on the creation of an area of 'freedom, security and justice' in the European Union, as last updated on 30 May 2002 (COM(2002) 261 final).

(¹²⁰) See point 2.15.1.

(¹²¹) See Council decision of 20 May 1999 determining, in conformity with the relevant provisions of the Treaty establishing the European Community and the Treaty on European Union, the legal basis for each of the provisions or decisions which constitute the Schengen acquis, OJ L 176, 10.7.1999, p. 17.

(¹²²) For example, Council framework decision of 15 March 2001 on the standing of victims in criminal proceedings (OJ L 82, 22.3.2001). A provision of this type is now systematically included in framework decisions proposed on the basis of Title VI of the EU Treaty. On 13 December 2001 the Commission presented a first report on the Council framework decision of 29 May 2000 on increasing protection by criminal penalties and other sanctions against counterfeiting in connection with the introduction of the euro (COM(2001) 771 final).

(¹²³) OJ C 364, 18.12.2000, p. 1.

move freely, to simplify Community legislation and to close certain loopholes, the Commission has tabled a proposal for a European Parliament and Council directive on the right of citizens of the Union and their family members to move and reside freely within the territory of the Member States (124). In this area, one particular infringement procedure merits special attention: on 19 September 2001 the Commission decided to refer to the Court of Justice a case involving the expulsion by Germany of Union citizens on public policy grounds.

The Court of Justice has on several occasions been asked to give preliminary rulings on restrictions on the free movement of persons on public policy grounds, but this is the first time an infringement procedure has been brought before it on this matter.

Following careful examination of the expulsion decisions and analysis of Germany's replies to the letter of formal notice and the reasoned opinion, the Commission felt that these expulsions revealed a variety of infringements by Germany of the EC Treaty and secondary legislation on the free movement of persons. The infringement, which affected both legislation and administrative practice, related in particular to the conditions of substance and form which Directive 64/221 requires Member States to observe when expelling a person who enjoys the protection of Community law.

The Commission decision follows on from its communication of 19 July 1999 (125) in which it drew attention to a number of points of vital interest regarding the interpretation of the provisions of Directive 64/221, such as respect for the principle of proportionality, the need to take account of all relevant factors in assessing the threat to public policy, the problem of the link under some legislative systems between a criminal conviction and expulsion, and the special situation of long-term residents.

2.16. BUDGET

The upward trend in infringement cases seen in earlier years has not continued, but the total number of disputes remains virtually unchanged.

2.16.1. Previously initiated proceedings

The Commission referred to the Court the case against the Netherlands (refusal to pay interest on late payment due under Article 11 of Council Regulation No 1552/89).

Since the correct application of the Community transit customs arrangements is a constant source of disputes with the Member States, the Commission decided to refer to the Court the case involving the incorrect clearance by the German authorities of Community transit documents.

2.16.2. New proceedings

The Commission decided to refer to the Court a test case which could be used as an example for resolving other cases involving the financial responsibility of the Member States for errors made during their management of own resources. In this case, the Danish authorities refused to accept financial responsibility for the loss of own resources resulting from an administrative error.

A reasoned opinion was sent to the French authorities following their refusal to reimburse VAT in connection with the application of the Protocol on Privileges and Immunities of the European Communities. The French authorities subsequently declared their intention of complying with the Commission's request. The Commission is waiting for the amounts requested to be actually paid before closing the infringement proceedings.

2.17. PERSONNEL AND ADMINISTRATION

The infringement procedures initiated by the Commission as regards the application of Community law to the Communities' staff concern the Member States' failure to comply with the Protocol on Privileges and Immunities of the European Communities and to implement national provisions required for the correct application of the Staff Regulations of Officials and the Conditions of Employment of Other Servants of the European Communities.

There are currently no ongoing infringement proceedings.

2.18. COMMUNITY STATISTICS

The reliability of Community statistics depends on Member States supplying the Commission with data relating to specific matters at predetermined intervals and by predetermined procedures.

No problems have been identified with the application of Community statistical legislation which would require the opening of an infringement procedure.

It should be noted that a complaint was received in 2000 about a Member State's alleged infringement of Community law, in particular Council Regulation (EC) No 3330/91 on the statistics relating to the trading of goods between Member States (Intrastat) and Council Decision 96/715/EC on inter-administration telematic networks for statistics relating to the trading of goods between Member States (Edicom). Following an analysis of the content the case was able to be shelved in 2001.

(124) OJ C 270E, 25.9.2001, p. 150.

(125) Cf. Communication from the Commission to the Council and the European Parliament on the special measures concerning the movement and residence of citizens of the Union which are justified on grounds of public policy, public security or public health, COM(1999)372 final.

ANNEX I

DETECTION OF INFRINGEMENT CASES

1.1. WAYS OF DETECTION OF INFRINGEMENT CASES

(situation as of 31 December 2001)

Year	Complaints (¹)	Cases detected by the Commission			Non communication (²)	Totaux
		Total	Parlementary questions	Petitions		
1996	819	257	22	4	1 079	2 155
1997	957	261	13	4	760	1 978
1998	1 128	396	18	7	610	2 134
1999	1 305	288	16	10	677	2 270
2000	1 225	313	15	5	896	2 434
2001	1 300	272	5	1	607	2 179

(¹) In 2001, 59.66 % of the infringement cases originated in complaints, as opposed to 50.32 % in 2000.

(²) Non communication: this category includes the non communication of national measures transposing Community directives, as well as the non communication of technical regulations under Directive 98/34/EC

1.2. CASES UNDER EXAMINATION (¹) BY THE COMMISSION AS OF 31 DECEMBER 2001, BY YEAR OF OPENING

Opened in		Under examination as of 31/12/2001		Complaints	Own initiative cases	Non-communication
			(%)			
2001	2 179	1 538	45.77	1 027	222	289
2000	2 434	768	23.00	471	179	118
1999	2 270	411	12.23	274	103	34
1998	2 134	2 55	7.59	118	110	27
1997	1 977	112	3.33	70	32	10
1996	2 151	72	2.14	36	32	4
1995	1 853	63	1.88	28	34	1
1994	2 396	47	1.40	15	29	3
1993	2 336	16	0.48	4	11	1
1992	2 509	11	0.33	5	6	0
1991	2 184	19	0.57	5	14	0
1990	2 343	19	0.57	6	13	0
1978-1989	8 049	29	0.86	1	28	0
Total	34 815	3 360	100.00	2 060	813	487

(¹) *The cases under examination are the cases opened following a complaint, an own Commission's initiative or a case of non-communication, whether or not an infringement procedure was initiated.*

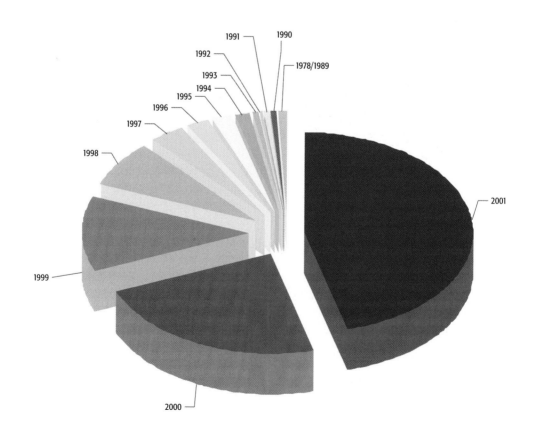

1.3. BREAKDOWN BY MEMBER STATE OF THE CASES OPENED IN 2001

1.3.1. Own initiative cases detected by the Commission in 2001, by Member State

Member State	Opened		Under exam. as of 31/12/2001	
		(%)		(%)
B	19	6.99	16	7.21
DK	7	2.57	5	2.25
D	10	3.68	8	3.60
EL	20	7.35	15	6.76
E	36	13.24	31	13.96
F	25	9.19	20	9.01
IRL	9	3.31	6	2.70
I	47	17.28	39	17.57
L	9	3.31	9	4.05
NL	9	3.31	7	3.15
A	21	7.72	18	8.11
P	15	5.51	12	5.41
FIN	22	8.09	18	8.11
S	13	4.78	11	4.95
UK	10	3.68	7	3.15
Total	272		222	

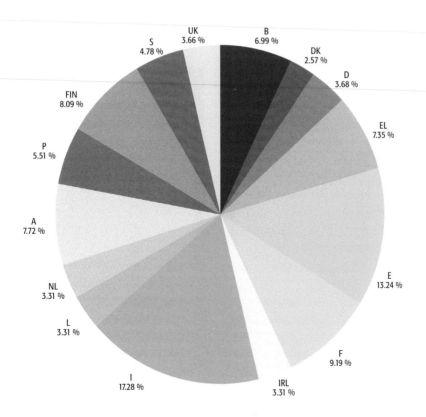

47

1.3.2. Complaints received in 2001, by Member State

Member State	Received	(%)	Cases under examination as of 31/12/2001	(%)
B	43	3.31	29	2.82
DK	91	7.00	26	2.53
D	181	13.92	148	14.41
EL	111	8.54	92	8.96
E	239	18.38	204	19.86
F	121	9.31	100	9.74
IRL	97	7.46	84	8.18
I	133	10.23	109	10.61
L	7	0.54	5	0.49
NL	31	2.38	28	2.73
A	39	3.00	33	3.21
P	36	2.77	31	3.02
FIN	39	3.00	27	2.63
S	46	3.54	41	3.99
UK	86	6.62	70	6.82
Total	1 300		1 027	

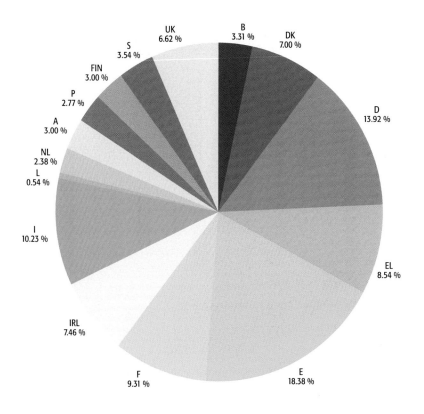

1.3.3. Non-communication cases opened in 2001, by Member State
(Non-communication of measures transposing directives and technical regulations
under Directive 98/34/EC)

Member State	Received		Cases under examination as of 31/12/2001	
		(%)		(%)
B	44	7.25	19	6.57
DK	28	4.61	7	2.42
D	45	7.41	20	6.92
EL	50	8.24	29	10.03
E	30	4.94	13	4.50
F	37	6.10	21	7.27
IRL	43	7.08	20	6.92
I	43	7.08	17	5.88
L	37	6.10	20	6.92
NL	42	6.92	16	5.54
A	46	7.58	27	9.34
P	50	8.24	26	9.00
FIN	33	5.44	15	5.19
S	35	5.77	14	4.84
UK	44	7.25	25	8.65
Total	607		289	

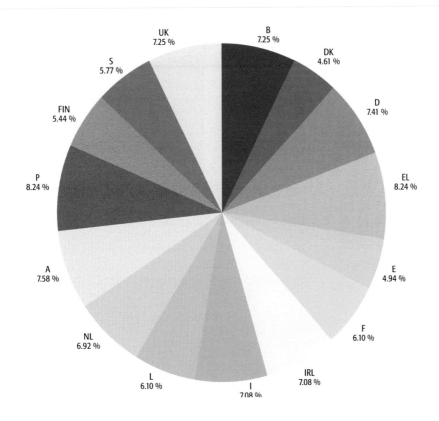

1.4. BREAKDOWN BY SECTOR OF THE CASES OPENED IN 2001

1.4.1. Own initiative cases detected by the Commission in 2001, by sector

Sector	Opened		Under examination as of 31/12/2001	
		(%)		(%)
Environment	111	40.81	91	40.99
Internal market	38	13.97	32	14.41
Health, Consumer protection	15	5.51	3	1.35
Enterprise	4	1.47	3	1.35
Taxation and Customs	9	3.31	9	4.05
Energy and Transport	10	3.68	9	4.05
Employment, Social affairs	10	3.68	10	4.50
Agriculture	6	2.21	5	2.25
Justice, Home affairs	3	1.10	2	0.90
Competition	3	1.10	3	1.35
Information society	29	10.66	24	10.81
Fisheries	15	5.51	15	6.76
Service juridique	0	0.00	0	0.00
Legal Service	8	2.94	8	3.60
Education and culture	5	1.84	3	1.35
Budget	5	1.84	4	1.80
Enlargement	0	0.00	0	0.00
Administration	0	0.00	0	0.00
Regional policies	1	0.37	1	0.45
Total	272		222	

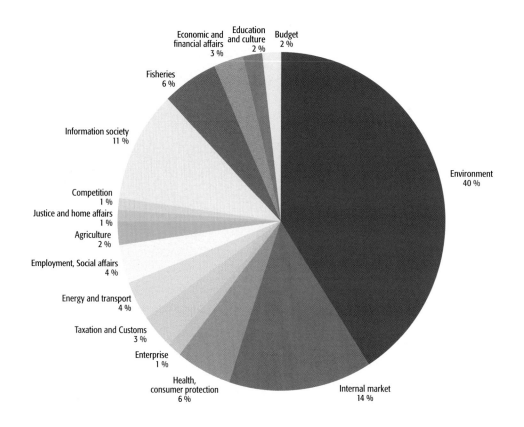

1.4.2. Complaints received in 2001, by sector

Sector	Opened	(%)	Under examination as of 31/12/2001	(%)
Environment	587	45.15	506	49.27
Internal market	351	27.00	231	22.49
Health, Consumer protection	86	6.62	73	7.11
Enterprise	16	1.23	14	1.36
Taxation and Customs	82	6.31	66	6.43
Energy and Transport	11	0.85	11	1.07
Employment, Social affairs	52	4.00	37	3.60
Agriculture	41	3.15	27	2.63
Justice, Home affairs	14	1.08	12	1.17
Competition	23	1.77	19	1.85
Information society	7	0.54	6	0.58
Fisheries	1	0.08	0	0.00
Legal Service	1	0.08	1	0.10
Economic and financial affairs	2	0.15	1	0.10
Education and culture	11	0.85	9	0.88
Budget	0	0.00	0	0.00
Enlargement	0	0.00	0	0.00
Administration	1	0.08	1	0.10
Regional policies	14	1.08	13	1.27
Total	1 300		1 027	

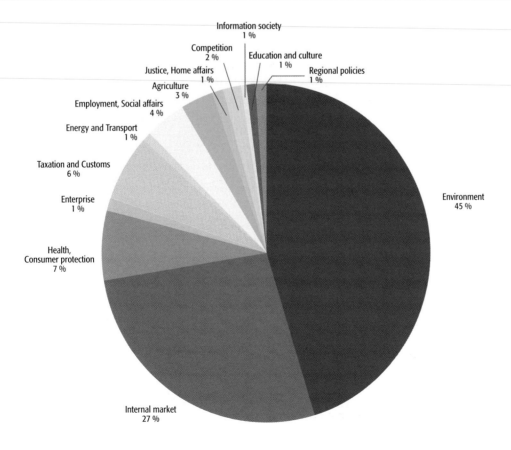

1.4.3. Non-communication cases opened in 2001, by sector

*(Non-communication of measures transposing directives and technical regulations
under Directive 98/34/EC*

Sector	Opened		Under examination as of 31/12/2001		Number of directives (adaptation term in 2001)	
		(%)		(%)		(%)
Environment	113	18.62	71	24.57	9	12.68
Internal market	45	7.41	29	10.03	4	5.63
Health, Consumer protection	233	38.39	70	24.22	26	36.62
Enterprise	107	17.63	52	17.99	16	22.54
Taxation and Customs	0	0.00	0	0.00	2	2.82
Energy and Transport	42	6.92	21	7.27	6	8.45
Employment, Social affairs	39	6.43	29	10.03	6	8.45
Agriculture (¹)	7	1.15	0	0.00	0	0.00
Competition	15	2.47	11	3.81	1	1.41
Information society	6	0.99	6	2.08	1	1.41
Total	607		289		71	

(¹) Relates to a directive for which the adaptation term was end 2000.

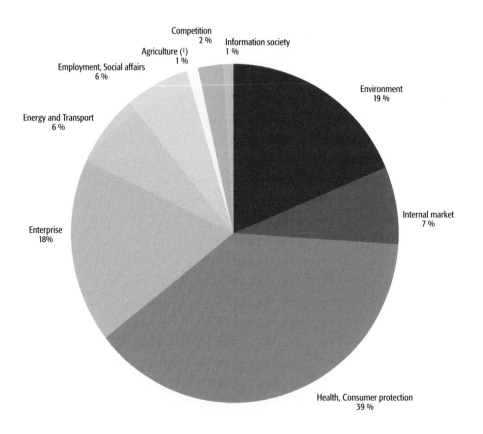

ANNEX II

INFRINGEMENT PROCEDURES — BREAK DOWN PER STAGE REACHED, LEGAL BASIS, MEMBER STATE AND SECTOR

2.1. ESTABLISHED INFRINGEMENTS — CLASSIFIED BY STAGE OF PROCEEDINGS AND MEMBER STATE

Member State	Letters of formal notice					Reasoned opinions					Referrals to Court				
	1997	1998	1999	2000	2001	1997	1998	1999	2000	2001	1997	1998	1999	2000	2001
B	93	88	80	92	87	33	78	30	34	44	18	20	15	5	13
DK	64	40	46	54	38	1	10	4	7	10	0	1	1	0	2
D	116	88	84	92	73	35	46	30	40	39	19	5	9	11	12
EL	109	95	88	115	83	23	51	48	35	71	10	16	14	23	16
E	104	78	72	93	65	23	36	21	32	37	7	6	7	8	14
F	157	121	86	110	74	49	94	61	43	50	15	23	35	27	22
IRL	86	63	67	91	80	14	46	32	27	50	6	10	15	17	13
I	123	110	85	118	96	36	91	41	50	53	20	16	32	24	22
L	74	62	65	78	50	14	39	38	40	33	8	11	18	16	10
NL	65	28	68	64	53	11	23	16	16	25	3	3	1	12	5
A	109	76	85	85	80	38	38	37	33	44	0	4	9	8	7
P	116	80	87	120	73	35	57	50	46	38	14	5	13	10	7
FIN	78	52	44	63	61	8	16	5	14	16	0	1	0	4	2
S	75	54	57	72	58	6	15	14	13	14	0	1	1	3	3
UK	92	66	61	70	79	8	35	33	30	45	1	1	8	4	14
Total	1 461	1 101	1 075	1 317	1 050	334	675	460	460	569	121	123	178	172	162

2.2. INFRINGEMENT PROCEEDINGS CLASSIFIED BY MEMBER STATE, STAGE REACHED AND LEGAL BASIS

		1997					1998				
		Total	Directives			Treaties, Regulations, Decisions	Total	Directives			Treaties, Regulations, Decisions
			No notification	Non conformity	Bad application			No notification	Non conformity	Bad application	
B	LFN	93	72	4	7	10	88	45	10	14	19
	RO	33	15	1	5	12	78	41	10	11	16
	REF	18	11	2	3	2	20	9	0	2	9
DK	LFN	64	53	6	2	3	40	28	1	3	8
	RO	1	0	0	1	0	10	4	2	2	2
	REF	0	0	0	0	0	1	0	0	0	1
D	LFN	116	71	12	22	11	88	43	8	21	16
	RO	35	22	4	5	4	46	21	7	9	9
	REF	19	12	2	4	1	5	1	0	3	1
EL	LFN	109	87	3	7	12	95	58	8	17	12
	RO	23	14	0	5	4	51	34	2	6	9
	REF	10	8	1	1	0	16	7	0	8	1
E	LFN	104	68	10	11	15	78	31	4	28	15
	RO	23	8	4	7	4	36	15	3	7	11
	REF	7	2	0	3	2	6	3	1	2	0
F	LFN	157	74	9	44	30	121	49	14	26	32
	RO	49	14	3	18	14	94	43	6	22	23
	REF	15	9	1	4	1	23	7	3	8	5
IRL	LFN	86	71	4	10	1	63	46	2	11	4
	RO	14	9	2	3	0	46	39	0	4	3
	REF	6	5	0	1	0	10	9	1	0	0
I	LFN	123	65	11	26	21	110	48	10	25	27
	RO	36	18	4	5	9	91	45	8	22	16
	REF	20	14	1	5	0	16	14	0	1	1
L	LFN	74	65	5	3	1	62	54	3	3	2
	RO	14	10	2	1	1	39	30	1	6	2
	REF	8	7	0	0	1	11	9	0	0	2
NL	LFN	65	46	4	9	6	28	15	2	6	5
	RO	11	3	1	5	2	23	12	3	3	5
	REF	3	1	0	2	0	3	0	0	3	0
A	LFN	109	85	4	11	9	76	43	14	11	8
	RO	38	33	0	4	1	38	25	3	6	4
	REF	0	0	0	0	0	4	1	0	2	1
P	LFN	116	85	7	18	6	80	53	5	12	10
	RO	35	18	6	5	6	57	37	5	10	5
	REF	14	7	5	2	0	5	0	0	2	3
FIN	LFN	78	64	2	8	4	52	29	7	9	7
	RO	8	8	0	0	0	16	8	1	6	1
	REF	0	0	0	0	0	1	0	0	0	1
S	LFN	75	58	8	4	5	54	34	7	6	7
	RO	6	6	0	0	0	15	8	2	2	3
	REF	0	0	0	0	0	1	0	0	0	1
UK	LFN	92	65	8	14	5	66	39	12	9	6
	RO	8	1	2	5	0	35	22	6	3	4
	REF	1	0	0	1	0	1	0	0	0	1
TOTAL	LFN	1 461	1 029	97	196	139	1 101	615	107	201	178
	RO	334	179	29	69	57	675	384	59	119	113
	REF	121	76	12	26	7	123	60	5	31	27

LFN: Letter of formal notice   RO: Reasoned opinion   REF: Referral to the Court

1999					2000					2001				
Total	Directives			Treaties, Regulations, Decisions	**Total**	Directives			Treaties, Regulations, Decisions	**Total**	Directives			Treaties, Regulations, Decisions
	No notification	Non conformity	Bad application			No notification	Non conformity	Bad application			No notification	Non conformity	Bad application	
80	43	10	13	14	92	64	6	11	11	87	44	1	23	19
30	13	6	6	5	34	14	6	8	6	44	25	7	7	5
15	5	5	2	3	5	3	1	1	0	13	6	4	3	0
46	32	4	4	6	54	45	2	3	4	38	28	2	3	5
4	3	0	0	1	7	1	3	1	2	10	3	2	4	1
1	0	1	0	0	0	0	0	0	0	2	0	0	1	1
84	47	7	21	9	92	51	7	23	11	73	44	0	24	5
30	12	5	8	5	40	20	4	11	5	39	22	4	9	4
9	4	1	1	3	11	4	2	4	1	12	4	4	4	0
88	60	4	12	12	115	89	4	10	12	83	50	3	18	12
48	29	6	7	6	35	24	2	5	4	71	54	1	8	8
14	11	1	2	0	23	18	1	2	2	16	12	1	3	0
72	40	5	16	11	93	46	4	31	12	65	30	2	27	6
21	4	4	11	2	32	10	1	14	7	37	16	4	14	3
7	2	4	1	0	8	2	1	3	2	14	6	0	7	1
86	46	3	12	25	110	64	8	17	21	74	36	7	21	10
61	21	11	24	5	43	20	6	3	14	50	21	4	13	12
35	13	2	9	11	27	11	5	6	5	22	12	3	5	2
67	45	3	14	5	91	69	0	20	2	80	42	2	24	12
32	22	4	4	2	27	17	2	6	2	50	31	2	13	4
15	10	1	2	2	17	13	1	2	1	13	10	1	2	0
85	57	4	19	5	118	61	15	30	12	96	44	6	31	15
41	21	8	7	5	50	24	4	17	5	53	23	8	17	5
32	15	4	5	8	24	6	5	6	7	22	8	5	5	4
65	48	10	4	3	78	67	1	6	4	50	37	4	3	6
38	33	5	0	0	40	24	7	6	3	33	25	2	4	2
18	16	2	0	0	16	13	0	3	0	10	3	2	3	2
68	50	2	6	10	64	44	3	13	4	53	41	2	5	5
16	13	0	2	1	16	8	2	3	3	25	15	2	7	1
1	0	1	0	0	12	9	1	2	0	5	0	2	0	3
85	49	12	7	17	85	61	13	9	2	80	47	13	13	7
37	24	4	5	4	33	15	6	3	9	44	26	11	6	1
9	7	2	0	0	8	5	1	0	2	7	3	3	0	1
87	63	4	12	8	120	97	3	16	4	73	49	2	14	8
50	37	4	5	4	46	31	4	10	1	38	24	1	10	3
13	7	3	2	1	10	8	0	0	2	7	4	0	3	0
44	36	2	3	3	63	57	2	3	1	61	41	10	3	7
5	0	3	2	0	14	8	3	1	2	16	12	3	1	0
0	0	0	0	0	4	0	0	4	0	2	2	0	0	0
57	44	6	5	2	72	56	3	3	10	58	36	5	7	10
14	7	4	2	1	13	8	4	1	0	14	5	1	5	3
1	0	1	0	0	3	2	0	1	0	3	1	2	0	0
61	46	2	7	6	70	54	5	7	4	79	46	3	23	7
33	21	4	5	3	30	19	1	8	2	45	32	4	7	2
8	5	1	0	2	4	1	0	2	1	14	11	1	1	1
1 075	706	78	155	136	1 317	925	76	202	114	1 050	615	62	239	134
460	260	68	88	44	460	243	55	97	65	569	334	56	125	54
178	95	29	24	30	172	95	18	36	23	162	82	28	37	15

2.2.1. Letters of formal notice sent in 2001, by legal basis and Member State

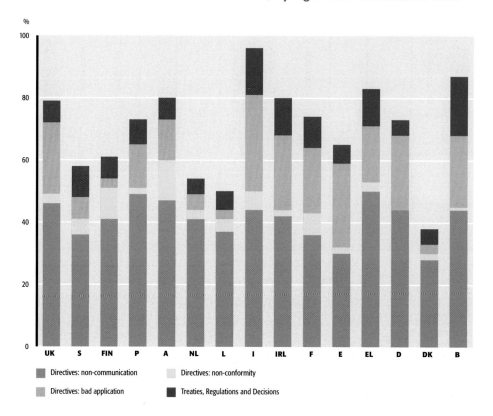

2.2.2. Reasoned opinions sent in 2001, by legal basis and Member State

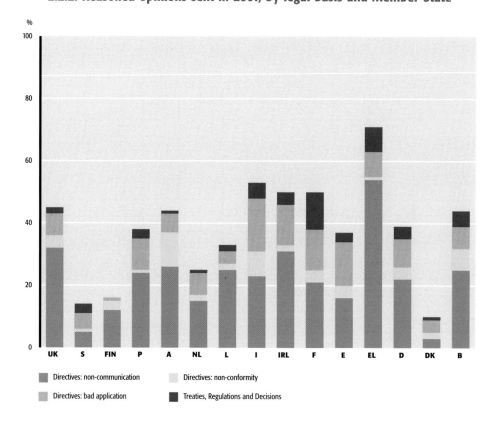

2.2.3. Referrals to the Court of justice in 2001, by legal basis and Member State

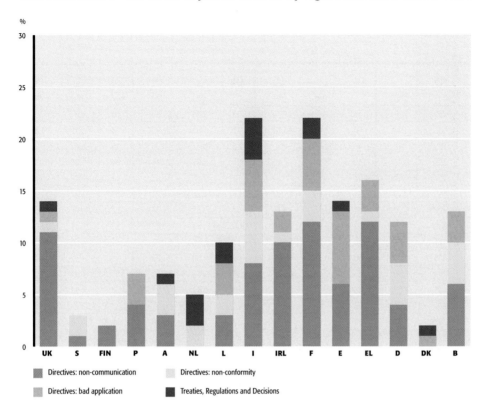

2.3. CASES UNDER EXAMINATION: PROCEDURE STATEMENT AS OF 31/12/2001, BY MEMBER STATE

Member State	Total	(%)	(1)	(%)	(2) (%)	(3)	(%)	(4) (%)	(5)	(%)	(6) (%)	(7)
B	189	5.63	136	8.15	71.96	68	7.28	35.98	23	6.63	12.17	6
DK	82	2.44	40	2.40	48.78	18	1.93	21.95	4	1.15	4.88	0
D	385	11.46	146	8.75	37.92	80	8.57	20.78	28	8.07	7.27	2
EL	295	8.78	140	8.39	47.46	81	8.67	27.46	34	9.80	11.53	5
E	487	14.49	132	7.91	27.10	70	7.49	14.37	26	7.49	5.34	2
F	355	10.57	191	11.44	53.80	125	13.38	35.21	53	15.27	14.93	13
IRL	199	5.92	94	5.63	47.24	52	5.57	26.13	27	7.78	13.57	5
I	380	11.31	182	10.90	47.89	106	11.35	27.89	57	16.43	15.00	7
L	81	2.41	70	4.19	86.42	47	5.03	58.02	17	4.90	20.99	2
NL	136	4.05	80	4.79	58.82	43	4.60	31.62	15	4.32	11.03	1
A	188	5.60	129	7.73	68.62	69	7.39	36.70	15	4.32	7.98	1
P	144	4.29	98	5.87	68.06	60	6.42	41.67	14	4.03	9.72	2
FIN	101	3.01	58	3.48	57.43	23	2.46	22.77	6	1.73	5.94	0
S	118	3.51	57	3.42	48.31	23	2.46	19.49	6	1.73	5.08	0
UK	220	6.55	116	6.95	52.73	69	7.39	31.36	22	6.34	10.00	1
Total	3 360		1 669		49.67	934		27.80	347		10.33	47

(1) Cases under examination as of 31 December 2001 for which the infringement procedure has been opened and percentages with regard to all the cases.

(2) Percentage of cases for which the infringement procedure has been opened with regard to cases under examination as of 31 December 2001 concerning this Member State.

(3) Cases for which a reasoned opinion has been sent and percentages with regard to all the cases.

(4) Percentage of cases for which a reasoned opinion has been sent with regard to all cases under examination as of 31 December 2001 concerning this Member State.

(5) Cases brought to the ECJ and percentages with regard to all cases.

(6) Percentage of cases referred to the ECJ with regard to all cases under examination as of 31 December 2001 for this Member State.

(7) Cases for which the procedure under Article 228 of the Treaty has been opened.

2.3.1. Cases under examination as of 31/12/2001 for which the infringement procedure has been opened by Member State

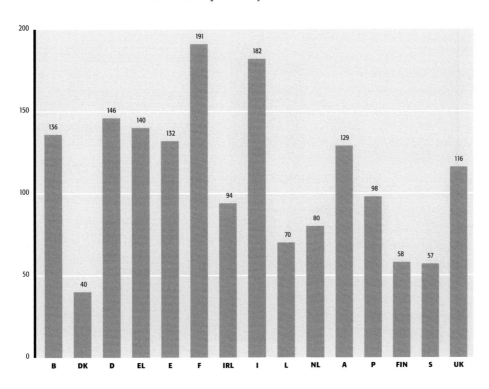

2.3.2. Cases under examination as of 31/12/2001, for which a reasoned opinion has been sent by Member State

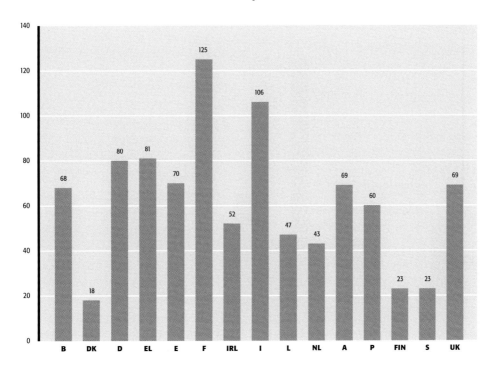

2.3.3. Cases under examination as of 31/12/2001 referred to the ECJ by Member State

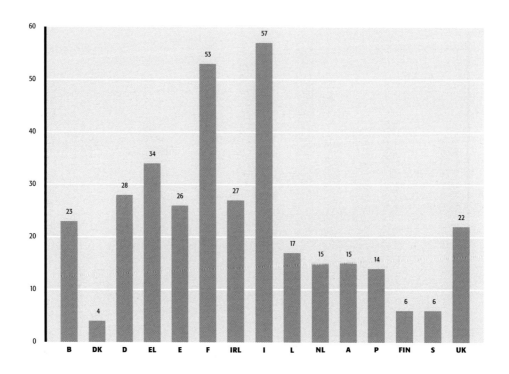

2.3.4. Cases under examination as of 31/12/2001, for which the 228 procedure has been opened by Member State

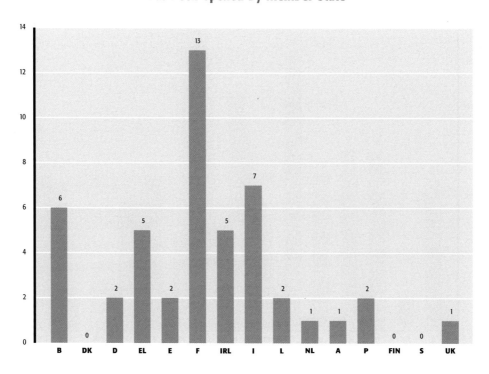

2.4. Cases under examination as of 31/12/2001, by sector

Secteur	Total	(%)	(1)	(%)	(2) (%)	(3)	(%)	(4) (%)	(5)	(%)	(6) (%)	(7)
Environment	1 302	38.75	488	29.24	37.48	293	31.37	22.50	127	36.60	9.75	20
Internal market	763	22.71	368	22.05	48.23	192	20.56	25.16	63	18.16	8.26	5
Agriculture	71	2.11	28	1.68	39.44	20	2.14	28.17	2	0.58	2.82	0
Entreprise	137	4.08	110	6.59	80.29	52	5.57	37.96	11	3.17	8.03	2
Social affairs	178	5.30	116	6.95	65.17	56	6.00	31.46	23	6.63	12.92	3
Customs and Taxation	217	6.46	113	6.77	52.07	63	6.75	29.03	23	6.63	10.60	1
Energy and Transport	128	3.81	111	6.65	86.72	86	9.21	67.19	43	12.39	33.59	10
Competition	59	1.76	22	1.32	37.29	9	0.96	15.25	4	1.15	6.78	0
Information society	69	2.05	53	3.18	76.81	25	2.68	36.23	6	1.73	8.70	1
Health, Consumer protection	249	7.41	152	9.11	61.04	95	10.17	38.15	27	7.78	10.84	4
Fisheries	47	1.40	44	2.64	93.62	18	1.93	38.30	6	1.73	12.77	1
Financial affairs	29	0.86	15	0.90	51.72	9	0.96	31.03	6	1.73	20.69	0
Budget	20	0.60	19	1.14	95.00	8	0.86	40.00	3	0.86	15.00	0
Education, culture, audiovisual	31	0.92	13	0.78	41.94	5	0.54	16.13	2	0.58	6.45	0
Administration	2	0.06	0	0.00	0.00	0	0.00	0.00	0	0.00	0.00	0
Enlargement	2	0.06	0	0.00	0.00	0	0.00	0.00	0	0.00	0.00	0
Regional policy	14	0.42	1	0.06	7.14	0	0.00	0.00	0	0.00	0.00	0
Justice and home affairs	40	1.19	16	0.96	40.00	3	0.32	7.50	1	0.29	2.50	0
Legal Service	2	0.06	0	0.00	0.00	0	0.00	0.00	0	0.00	0.00	0
Total	3 360		1 669		49.67	934		27.80	347		10.33	47

(1) Cases under examination as of 31 December 2001 for which the infringement procedure has been opened and percentages with regard to all the cases.

(2) Percentage of cases for which the infringement procedure has been opened with regard to cases under examination as of 31 December 2001 concerning this sector.

(3) Cases for which a reasoned opinion has been sent and percentages with regard to all the cases.

(4) Percentage of cases for which a reasoned opinion has been sent with regard to all cases under examination as of 31 December 2001 concerning this sector.

(5) Cases brought to the ECJ and percentages with regard to all cases.

(6) Percentage of cases referred to the ECJ with regard to all cases under examination as of 31 December 2001 for this sector.

(7) Cases for which the procedure under article 228 of the Treaty has been opened.

2.4.1. Cases under examination as of 31/12/2001 for which infringement procedure has been opened, by sector

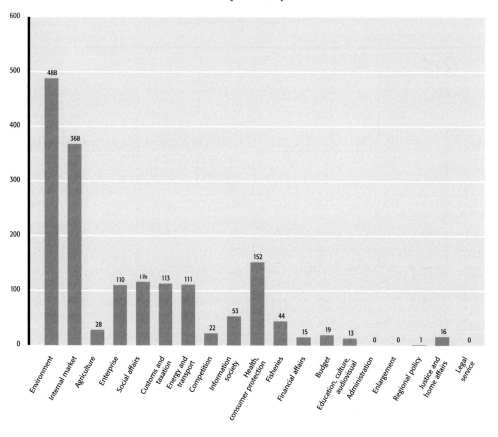

2.4.2. Cases under examination as of 31/12/2001 for which a reasoned opinion has been sent, by sector

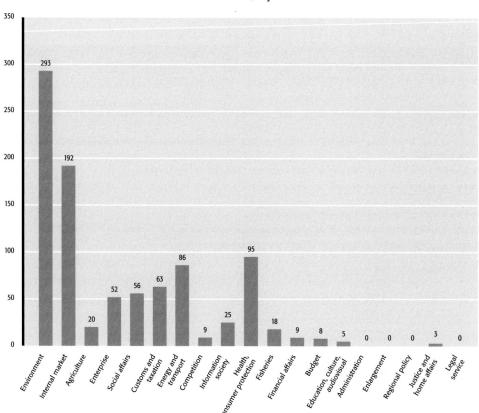

2.4.3. Cases under examination as of 31/12/2001 referred to the Court of Justice, by sector

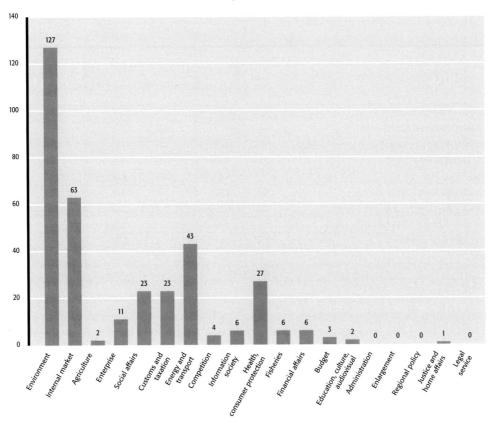

2.4.4. Cases under examination as of 31/12/2001 for which a procedure ex article 228 has been initiated, by sector

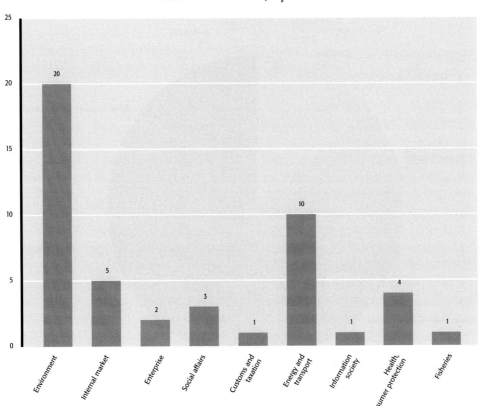

2.5. CASES CLOSED IN 2001

By stage			Non-communication		Except non-communication	
		(%)		(%)		(%)
Before sending a letter of formal notice	792	41.36	2	0.26	790	68.64
Before sending a reasoned opinion	684	35.72	502	65.71	182	15.81
Before deciding to bring the case to the ECJ	173	9.03	114	14.92	59	5.13
Before the referral to the ECJ	122	6.37	70	9.16	52	4.52
Withdrawal	75	3.92	53	6.94	22	1.91
Before sending the Article 228 formal notice	52	2.72	18	2.36	34	2.95
Before sending the Article 228 reasoned opinion	10	0.52	4	0.52	6	0.52
Before deciding to bring the 228 case to the ECJ	3	0.16	1	0.13	2	0.17
Before the 228 referral to the ECJ	1	0.05	0	0.00	1	0.09
Withdrawal	3	0.16	0	0.00	3	0.26
Total	1 915		764		1 151	

2.5.1. Cases closed in 2001, by stage

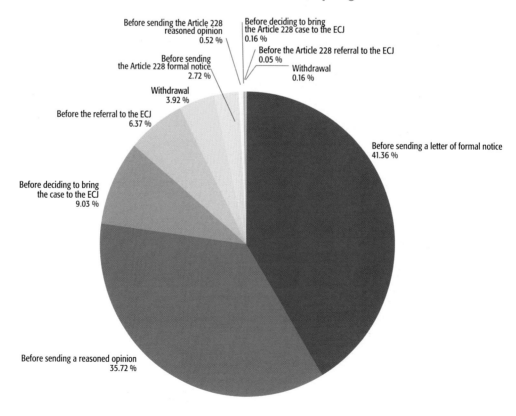

2.5.2. Cases closed in 2001, non-communication, by stage

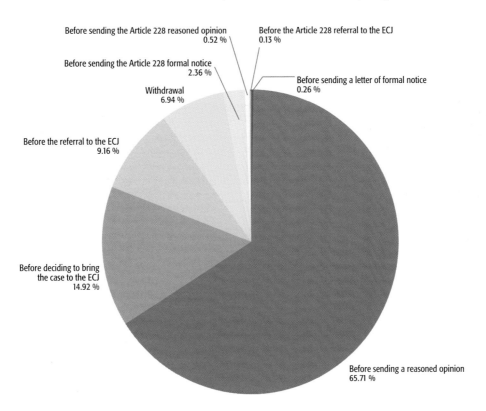

Before sending the Article 228 reasoned opinion
0.52 %

Before the Article 228 referral to the ECJ
0.13 %

Before sending the Article 228 formal notice
2.36 %

Before sending a letter of formal notice
0.26 %

Withdrawal
6.94 %

Before the referral to the ECJ
9.16 %

Before deciding to bring
the case to the ECJ
14.92 %

Before sending a reasoned opinion
65.71 %

2.5.3. Cases closed in 2001 except non-communication, by stage

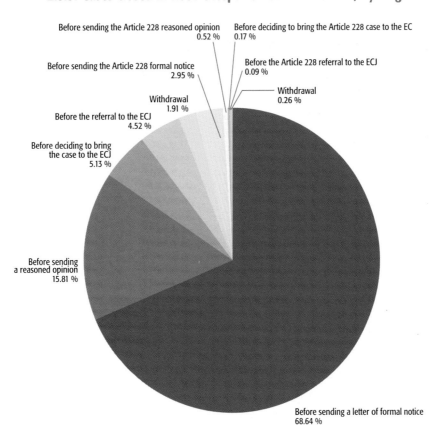

Before sending the Article 228 reasoned opinion
0.52 %

Before deciding to bring the Article 228 case to the EC
0.17 %

Before sending the Article 228 formal notice
2.95 %

Before the Article 228 referral to the ECJ
0.09 %

Withdrawal
1.91 %

Withdrawal
0.26 %

Before the referral to the ECJ
4.52 %

Before deciding to bring
the case to the ECJ
5.13 %

Before sending
a reasoned opinion
15.81 %

Before sending a letter of formal notice
68.64 %

2.6. EVOLUTION OF THE CLOSURE DECISIONS

Year	Total of the closure decisions	Closure of an opened infringement procedure
2001	1 915	*1 133*
2000	1 899	*1 165*
1999	1 900	*1 138*
1998	1 961	*1 282*
1997	2 112	*1 494*
1996	1 483	*670*

European Commission

Nineteenth annual report on monitoring the application of Community law 2001

Luxembourg: Office for Official Publications of the European Communities

2002 — 66 pp. — 21 x 29.7 cm

ISBN 92-894-4114-3

Price (excluding VAT) in Luxembourg: EUR 34